HERE BE DRAGONS

HONG
HERE BE DRAGONS
KONG

Edited by Rick Browne and James Marshall
Essay by Simon Winchester

STEWART, TABORI & CHANG
NEW YORK

PAGES 2 AND 3: View over Hong Kong toward Kowloon and the New Territories (James Marshall).

PAGES 4 AND 5: The Kwai Chung Container Port (Alex Webb).

PAGES 6 AND 7: Deep Bay cultivators raise fish in cages suspended from floating platforms near the Chinese border (Jodi Cobb).

PAGE 8: I. M. Pei's Bank of China building towers over Hong Kong's Legislative Council building (James Marshall).

PAGE 9: Dragon mural in Star Ferry terminal (Rob Nelson).

PAGE 11: Hong Kong parade (Neil Farrin).

"Here Be Dragons" essay copyright © 1992 Simon Winchester.

All other text copyright © 1992 Rick Browne and James Marshall.

Photograph on page 111 copyright © 1992 Steve Stroud.

All other photographs copyright © 1992 individual photographers as noted specifically on page 240, which constitutes an extension of this page.

Published in 1992 by Stewart, Tabori & Chang, Inc. 575 Broadway, New York, New York 10012

Library of Congress Cataloguing-in-Publication Data
Winchester, Simon.
    Hong Kong : here be dragons / edited by Rick Browne and James Marshall ; essay by Simon Winchester.
    Includes index.
    ISBN 1-55670-249-3
    1. Hong Kong—Description and travel—Views.
I. Browne, Rick. II. Marshall, James, 1955–
III. Title.
DS796.H743W56   1992
951.25—dc20   91-37805
                              CIP

Distributed in the U.S. by Workman Publishing, 708 Broadway, New York, New York 10003

Distributed in Canada by Canadian Manda Group, P.O. Box 920 Station U, Toronto, Ontario M8Z 5P9

Distributed in all other territories by Little, Brown and Company, International Division, 34 Beacon Street, Boston, Massachusetts 02108

Captions by Judy Jacobs
Design by Diana M. Jones
Map by Guenter Vollath
Printed in Hong Kong
10 9 8 7 6 5 4 3 2 1
First Edition

HERE BE DRAGONS
PROJECT STAFF

PICTURE EDITORS,
HONG KONG
*Dubravka Bondulic, Patricia Davis,
Steve Stroud*

PICTURE EDITOR,
NEW YORK
Guy Cooper

LOGISTICS MANAGERS
Emmy Lung, Wendy Lo

PRODUCTION ASSISTANTS
*Edmund Chan, Akin Lai, Ivan Lau,
and Michael Yueng*

OFFICE ASSISTANT
Dorothy Chan Lai Lai

PROJECT DOCUMENTARY
PHOTOGRAPHER
Baron Kam

VIDEOGRAPHER
Dean Head

CONTENTS

Trams on Kings Road in Causeway Bay (Susan Biddle).

::

PAGES 14 AND 15: A woman flies her kite (Neil Farrin).

This book has
been made possible
by the generous assistance
of the following
American and
Hong Kong corporations:

PREFACE

WE FIRST CONCEIVED of bringing a group of photojournalists together to make a book that would capture the "spirit of Hong Kong" while we were both on assignment covering Hong Kong's International Dragon Boat Festival in 1987. Our dream began to take shape the following year, during the Chinese Lunar Year of the Dragon. Since then, after what seems like hundreds of meetings in which we sought to convince others of the seriousness of our intent, we have repeated that phrase, "spirit of Hong Kong," endlessly, almost as if it were a mantra.

What we shared during the early stages of our venture was a vivid infatuation with this enthralling Asian city, which, in reality, neither of us then knew particularly well. But we did know one thing clearly: that we wanted to learn more. We wanted to understand the magnetic attraction that we felt for this place.

Later, while trying to find a title that would express our ambitions for this book, we happened upon the phrase "here be dragons," an inscription on old European maps of the China

coast. To early mapmakers, the area was the unknown, and the unknown was to be feared; the dragon of European mythology was a gruesome creature that represented the mapmakers' apprehensions about unexplored places. In contrast, we soon learned, the dragon of the Orient embodies "the genius of strength and goodness. He is the spirit of change," according to the writer Okakura (*Awakening of Japan*, 1904).

It struck us that this old map inscription might well relate to our own enterprise. We, too, were explorers from foreign lands. But, unlike our predecessors, we did not fear this unknown place. What we sensed in "the spirit of Hong Kong" was a less tangible dragon: its strength, the tenacity of its people, and, especially in these times, its adaptability to change. Through our project, we hoped to uncover the workings of Hong Kong and thereby come to understand the "dragons" of this culture. We decided to adopt "Here Be Dragons" as our project name.

Along the way we have met hundreds of people, individuals from every walk of life, from the titans of Hong Kong's formidable industry, to residents of its prestigious "Peak" district, to still others who labor in meager quarters in pursuit of the Hong Kong dream of prosperity. Each has provided us with insights and, in doing so, has allowed us slowly though surely to become a part of Hong Kong. We are pleased, here, to present the results of our experience.

In June of 1989, well into developing the project, we watched in horror with the rest of the world the terrible events of Tiananmen Square. Beyond the tragedy unfolding in Beijing, an immediate awareness rippled throughout the world: 1997, the date Hong Kong would be reunified with China. It was a side issue at the time, but one with heavy consequences. As the summer progressed, we watched 1997's shadow on Hong Kong's future grow longer. Given the magnitude of the shocking events in China, we realized that our attempt to capture the "spirit of Hong Kong" was vital. Our resolve to create this book was set: Hong Kong's story had gained considerable urgency.

The photographs on these pages present Hong Kong today, a city vibrant with life. They show the tenacity of Hong Kong's people, their strength of purpose, and fierce devotion to work and family. Our intent is to call attention to a special and unique way of life that could so easily be lost through poor stewardship. Our hope is that each reader of this book will be compelled to ask, "What will Hong Kong be like in the future?" By doing so, we might collectively challenge the arbitrators of its future to answer that question with respect for human dignity and in keeping with the terms of their agreement.

The work of our team of photojournalists speaks for itself. For ten days in January of 1991, they came to this peninsula (and these islands) and did what they do best—told its story through dynamic photography. They have contributed their hearts, minds, and eyes to produce what we feel is the most intimate, honest, and realistic look at Hong Kong ever published.

Many of the images in this book are strong and frank. We do not believe that well-being or continued prosperity can be ensured merely through the power of suggestion. Not all that we found, or show herein, is grand and glorious, but we are confident that strength lies in the truth. In this regard our strongest gratitude must be directed to the community of American and Hong Kong corporations who believed in and stood behind the integrity of our vision, and made it possible for us to tell our story.

To us this book is much more than just individual fractions of time stolen from history and recorded in ink on paper. We hope that these images will instill the same fascination in those who study these pages that we first felt standing in the midst of the mesmerizing tapestry that is Hong Kong. We seek to present this vision to a waiting and concerned world. As Laurence Durrell once wrote, "the final measure of the spirit of a place is the people who inhabit it." We thank the people of Hong Kong for letting us into their lives. It is to them, and to their enduring spirit, that we dedicate this book.

Rick Browne
SCOTTS VALLEY, CALIFORNIA

James Marshall
MONTCLAIR, NEW JERSEY

OCTOBER 1991

*PAGES 18 AND 19: Fish farms near the Chinese border
(Jodi Cobb).*

17

HERE BE DRAGONS

Simon Winchester

A T FIRST BLUSH—from the air, perhaps, or from the deck of an approaching liner—Hong Kong looks to be a domain of the almost unrelieved perpendicular. Whole forests of blinding white skyscrapers soar from the coastal flats; solitary giants cling precariously to the hillsides, from the towers of new government cities in the far north to the rows of mighty apartment blocks in Repulse Bay in the far south. It sometimes seems as though no city on earth, aside from Manhattan, has such a concentration of verticality. Yet, as with

so much in Hong Kong, you look a little closer, and the image blurs, and changes.

Peer at the hillsides themselves, thick with tropical grasses and creepers and torn with deep fissures and crevices. Streams course down some of them; others are dry. And wedged into these latter, often spilling out of them into the woods like some kind of luxuriant equatorial growth, are scores upon scores of small wood-and-paper shacks. These are the dwelling places for an invisible, but far from insubstantial, population of Hong Kong, a people for whom power and piped water and income tax forms—

View of Central District and Wanchai from the esplanade at the Cultural Centre in Tsim Sha Tsui (Basil Pao).

■■

FACING PAGE:
The Island Eastern Corridor skirts the office buildings and housing projects of North Point in Hong Kong (Jodi Cobb).

and an address—are distant and often un-
wanted luxuries.

The Hong Kong government calls them
squatters. In Cantonese they are known as *shim
jin*—illegal settlers. But legal or not, seen or
unseen, it is these people, some of the half-
million old men and women from Hong Kong's
squatter communities, who start the rhythm
of each colonial day. For when the old Royal
Observatory, far away on Mount Elgin in
Kowloon, sounds the electronic pips that mark
four o'clock in the morning, a goodly number of
this unsung population is already on the move,

climbing up the hillsides for the customary
Buddhist observance of the rising of the sun.

Naturally, the time that this happens depends upon the season, though Hong Kong's
low latitude, just a little south of the Tropic of
Cancer, means that the annual variation is quite
modest. In winter the sun may rise a little after
six. In summer—and the dominant image of
Hong Kong surely has to be that of summer,
with all the heat, humidity, and those dawns
coming "up like thunder outer China" across the
sea—it does so around five. The matutinal pil-
grimage begins an hour earlier, while it is still
dark. One can hear the pilgrims calling to one
another like birds, checking that their familiar
though unseen friends are picking their ways
steadily and safely through the gloom. "*Josan!*"
they cry. "Good morning! Are you well?"

On the country paths near Mount Collinson, below the cluster of Cable & Wireless
receiving antennas, one can invariably hear and
then see scores of these dawn-walkers. Some
have been performing their quotidian ritual for
decades and have constructed a show of its near
permanence. Occasionally, off to one side of a
path such as Sir Cecil's Ride (named for where
a governor, Cecil Clementi, liked to take his
pony), you can find a flight of stone steps and,
at the top, a tiny garden that a group of old people laid out long ago, with flowers and a small
patch of scrubby lawn. It belongs to no one, and
yet it belongs to all.

By five o'clock there may be a small gather-

*Border fence between the Colony of Hong Kong and
the People's Republic of China at Lo Wu (Basil Pao).*

ing of friends sitting there beside the flowers, drinking tea and chattering noisily about the weather. Then comes the moment all have been awaiting, when the first orange lip of the sun appears on

triggers one thousand selenium cells on one thousand powerful arc lights, all of which promptly switch themselves off. The lights are on top of an immense, twenty-four-mile-long fence

the eastern horizon, and the South China Sea suddenly turns pale orange, and the stars wink out, and all Hong Kong appears below, bathed in the pastel glimmer of early dawn. At this moment, and for a few minutes more, the watchers fall silent, gazing in some kind of Buddhist rapture.

But their quiet lasts only a short while. Within moments, they resume their noisy banter, having satisfactorily ushered in another day, having prepared themselves spiritually to eke it out on the fringes—for the Hong Kong squatters are far from being a central part—of Her Britannic Majesty's only remaining colony in Asia.

IT SEEMS much more of a colony in the north. Far up there—or as far as it is possible to go in so tiny an enclave, in fact a mere twenty miles as the crow flies—the first glimmer of dawn

of steel and razor-wire that was erected along the Chinese border by the British army a dozen years ago. It was put up in an attempt to keep out those Chinese who might wish to try to migrate into the already overcrowded territory.

It is a fence as ugly as it is impressive—the more so since it shares the distinction of being one of only two Iron Curtains that remain in 1991 on the face of the earth (the other being that dividing North and South Korea). Some think it droll to learn that, in an age when barriers are being torn down and ideologies blurred all over the world, the government of Hong Kong still maintains a fence around itself, preserving and guarding its privileges and forbidding its neighbors to share in them. The colony, considered thus, seems rather like one of those exclusive and forbidding housing estates in Bel Air, where dogs and private security firms are hired to keep out those too poor to have any business there.

Shen Zhen Special Economic Zone, just over the
Hong Kong border in the People's Republic (Basil Pao).

For it is an observable fact that many southern Chinese—the same people, after all, who flooded into the enclave twenty and thirty years ago and, essentially, provided the colony with the labor force that has helped make it what it is today—are still trying to get in. Life in southern China remains horribly poor and repressed (though it is marginally better than that endured in northern China), and the inhabitants know only too well of the opportunities for wealth and comfort that lie beyond the arc lights and the barbed wire snaking to the south of the Shen Zhen River.

They can see the lights of the apartment blocks at night. They can even see the office skyscrapers. They can hear the radio news and pop songs. They can watch Hong Kong television, with all those commercials for Rolex watches and fine cognac and holidays in Thailand. They see and hear, in other words, temptation. And not altogether surprisingly, given the human propensity for self-betterment, a fair number of them each night try to get in—to cut the fence, to swim the bays, to struggle through the marshes, to evade the dogs, to climb through the barbed wire, and to avoid the platoons of Nepalese mercenary soldiers, the Gurkhas, whom the British authorities still employ to help them police the terrain of this wild and difficult frontier.

And each night a few lucky or skillful men (and a tiny number of lucky and skillful women) do manage to get through, and some of them even make it into the seething alleys of Sham Shui Po or Mong Kok or, by way of tunnel or ferry, to Hong Kong Island itself. There they vanish, emerging to take illicit jobs in cheap chicken restaurants or on building sites, each first living as a squatter while saving the first few dollars. Before long, though, the escapee will move into one of the hundreds of terrible rooms that can be found, filled with coffin-sized, rentable iron cages—a place to live, sort of, while earning a little more, before moving on and up to a hot and damp and tiny shared apartment, then buying a first pair of jeans, then getting that first Big Mac for dinner, then a small radio set—starting to clamber up, in other words, the precarious ladder of ambition that is presented by Hong Kong and that has been so steadfastly denied by China.

These immigrants are in Hong Kong illegally, of course. They have no identity cards, which a Hong Kong policeman has a perfect right to demand, with neither pretext nor warning. They risk being tossed out. They are often caught. But there are amnesties from time to time, and even if a hapless Cantonese is found out and returned to Canton, there is the consolation of having tasted the good life for a while, of having earned a few convertible dollars, and of having had some fun. Besides, one can always make another try: the British army says that there are so many frequent fliers across the fence that they appear to have been issued season tickets.

Most, however, do not get past the fence. All manner of electronic wizardry lies buried in the earth. The fence is alive with detection equipment. There are watchtowers, just as in old Berlin (though, to be fair, no guns are carried, and would-be emigrants do not face the likelihood of being shot). Posses of Gurkhas, many of them riding mountain bikes, patrol a path beside the fence, and there are fast all-terrain vehicles and helicopters and, as of 1990, specially trained policemen and auxiliaries too, all bent upon protecting the imperial integrity of this twenty-four-mile divide.

The results of their endeavors can be seen each dawn, once the fence lights click off and the would-be emigrants have decided to put off any further attempts for another night. At each of the army bases and police stations along the border, small groups of tired, wet, dirty, and frightened young Chinese men, each with his hands cuffed behind his back, are assembled by their captors. Each station's haul for the night is tabulated by policemen wearing rubber gloves, and each man is washed and given a rough-and-ready breakfast of tea and bread, perhaps a bowl of rice porridge if he is lucky.

The totals of each morning's haul are then telephoned down to the office of the police commander of the Frontier District, as well as to the headquarters of the British Forces. Officers of both services will talk idly of the past night's tally over their bacon and eggs, as they would talk of the weather or a show on television back home.

"Gather we got eighty-six eye-eyes last night," they might say, an eye-eye being an illegal immigrant. "Getting rather cheeky on the other side, I'd say. Wonder what they're after now?"

For it is usually *something*—a rumor of a new building site on which work can be found or of an exceptionally good horse running at the Sha Tin track or that another amnesty is expected soon and anyone who "touches base"—manages to climb the fence and evade capture and get into the city proper—will be allowed to stay. That was the policy in the seventies: the government ended it abruptly, saying that if it had remained policy, all of Hong Kong would now have the population density of Mong Kok, which the record books say is the world's most crowded place.

But come dawn and the state of alert at the frontier relaxes somewhat. The weary soldiers of the night are replaced by fresh patrols, whose duties are light and comprise what the British still call "a cushy number."

The reverse is true back in the colony itself, however: the light of early dawn is bringing to life the first signs of the energy for which Hong Kong is so rightly renowned. The first trains of the subway system begin swishing their way down from their depots shortly before six. The day's first expresses for China are being readied in Kowloon terminal (and it is perhaps worth remembering that, from the buffers in Kowloon, it is entirely possible to journey all the way to London, via Canton, Peking, Ulan

Bator, Irkutsk, Novosibirsk, Moscow, Berlin, and Amsterdam, to bump softly against the buffers of Liverpool Street Station). The venerable trams that rattle their one-dollar ways from the east end of Hong Kong Island to the west—"the man on the Shau Kei Wan tram" being the local equivalent of the rest of the world's man on the street—lurch out of their home among the tenements of Causeway Bay shortly thereafter.

AMONG THE GREAT BANK TOWERS of central Hong Kong—the district is officially called Victoria, named for the queen during whose reign the territory enjoyed more than a third of its total colonial existence—the morning's newspapers are being distributed in a marvelously frantic and haphazard ritual that could only happen, one suspects, in this particular town.

Fully a hundred yards of Queen's Road, between the Hongkong and Shanghai Bank building and that of the old Bank of China— where there is the newly built China Club offering "congee and oil-sticks" breakfasts and a magnificent library of ten thousand books to such Chinese businessmen who are willing to fork over the $20,000 membership fee—is closed off. Delivery vans from the various newspaper publishers—this is a colony that supports more than forty daily newspapers (London, so fabled a bastion of free speech, has but a dozen, and New York, four)—are lined up along the road.

Strong-shouldered young men are tossing

bundles of newspapers down to those who will sell them during the day: old ladies with iron-wheeled carts they will tug all the way up to Old Bailey or Ladder Street; middle-aged men in old cars who have secured the right to deliver to blocks of apartments in the Mid-Levels, where the wealthier *gweilos*, the white ghosts, the

barbarian foreigners like to live; thin old men who take a few copies of the racing papers to try to sell later in the day outside the Royal Hong Kong Jockey's Club's betting shops, perhaps making a few dollars peddling advice on which nag to back in the eight-fifteen.

At half-past five the street is crowded with

Central District trolley (Rick Browne).

vans and carts and awash in newspaper litter. But by six, by some mysterious act that no one ever seems to report seeing, all the vehicles, all the people, and most remarkable, all of the waste paper have vanished. It is as though the ritual had never happened. The copies of the *South China Morning Post* or *Ming Pao* or the *Economic Journal* or one of the communist papers that appear beneath your doorway or at the corner stands seem to have done so as if by magic.

The newspaper business has another mysterious and typically Hong Kong side to it as well —and one for which the first of the daily delivery vehicles will shortly arrive. Out at Kai Tak Airport, some of the women who clean the incoming planes—all of which, of course, arrive from abroad, since the colony is far too tiny to sport an internal air service—ferret out all the crumpled newspapers, those from London or Paris or Frankfurt or New York—press them flat with a steam iron, fold them presentably once again, and offer them for sale. It is profitable, freelance, inventive, surprising, and slightly illicit—a nice metaphor for the kind of close-to-the-wind money-making adventurism for which the colony is famous.

Within an hour or so of the arrival of an inbound jet, copies of the papers that it carried are on sale in Kowloon; they'll be on sale over on the Hong Kong side half an hour later. Once in a while the ladies err. A copy of the previous day's London *Times* was once handed to a delighted hotel guest at breakfast. While he was eating his kipper, he discovered, to his great dismay, that someone, presumably a passenger on the plane about whose existence he was not supposed to know, had completed the crossword. He mentioned it to the waiter.

"Perhaps you may be a little vexed, sir," the man replied, with magisterial grandeur. "But it simply demonstrates the exceptionally high level of service in Hong Kong: for our most distinguished guests we even do your crossword for you."

In theory, were this a perfectly reliable system for the delivery of foreign papers, the first to hit the colony's streets each day should be the *San Francisco Examiner*. The first plane

Cityplaza Ice Palace in Cityplaza Mall,
in Quarry Bay (Alex Webb).

27

each morning comes from across the Pacific: Singapore Airlines Flight 001, nonstop from San Francisco and scheduled to arrive after the morning's noise-abatement curfew lifts at

6:30 A.M. It is the first of the day's three hundred aircraft movements, sixteen an hour, which stretch the colony's single runway to capacity and bring passengers directly from and take them directly to both the prosaic—London, Auckland, Los Angeles, Paris—and the more exotic—Colombo, Guilin, Muscat, and Kathmandu.

The plane's approach—if the air traffic controllers in the tower permit a landing from the northwest, on what is designated Runway 13—remains one of the world's most spectacular and, for those who are arriving in Hong Kong for the first time, the most heart-stopping.

The inbound jet flies along a track that is well to the south of Hong Kong Island. Passengers sitting on the right-hand side will be the first to perceive that the colony is near. The sea below, until now quite empty, suddenly comes alive with big ships churning their

way to and from somewhere, and there are schools of small fishing smacks trawling on the banks. Then appears the first of hundreds of tiny, sea-washed granite skerries, one, a long lozenge of an island topped by a still-winking lighthouse: Waglan Island, "the light at the end of the empire."

Next, with a rush, the green mass of Hong Kong Island itself rises from the sea, and a blurred mass of images flashes by below. First a forest of radar dishes and receiving antennas. Then a clutch of ramshackle villages, rocky beaches, and the first of dozens of tower blocks and developments that, from this height, resemble villas in the south of Spain. Then there is Stanley Barracks and the army parade ground, a secure-looking typhoon shelter for small ships, and the first of the greasy factories at Aberdeen; then the giant roller coaster at Ocean Park, the tiny temple down on Lamma Island, a power station that, your neighbor tells you, apocryphally, once had five chimneys—not the four originally planned—since the local Chinese regard the number four as unlucky, it being pronounced very much like the Cantonese

Dusk over Kowloon and Kai Tak Airport
(Neil Farrin).

word for death; and then a range of hills ahead, high and tipped with clouds.

As the plane inches steadily lower, the images below magnify at an equal rate. It has now well overshot Hong Kong itself, and

were it to head straight on, it would graze the high hills of Lantau Island and perhaps strike the world's biggest and grandest statue of the Lord Buddha, which local monks have recently set up on its plinth on a hillside by the Po Lin Monastery (the bronze Buddha was made by a Chinese ceramics plant that normally makes nose cones for the satellite-carrying rockets launched from Lop Nor Desert).

But SQ 001's destination is not Lantau (though future aircraft's will be, since the new airport, due in 1997, is being built on a small island off the northern Lantau coast). The jet thus makes a long and lazy right turn above a beacon on the hourglass-shaped Cheung Chau (an island with a number of small hotels, most notorious for weekend assignations) and heads back toward the Kowloon side of the territory, first speeding above the massive container terminal at Kwai Chung, which vies with

Rotterdam, Singapore, and New York to be the busiest in the world (and often wins, though for now it is second).

The city is hurtling upward now, and the buildings below are getting larger and ever larger. Old men, imprudently close, can be seen reading newspapers on the roofs of their buildings. Children playing outside their schools look up and clap their hands over their ears—as, if they are able, do countless housewives who are hanging wash out on bamboo poles run out from countless windows. The giant machine thunders ever downward and then, suddenly, it makes a steep right turn—of forty-seven degrees, in fact—such that its wing seems ready to scrape a thousand television antennas and a good deal else from the roofs of that vast and lawless slum known as the Walled City, which the government is now tearing down—unless a jet gets to it first.

But, of course—or, at least, one hopes that "of course" will always be the phrase; some pilots say they rather doubt it—the jet manages to sing straight past and then to straighten up and finally touch down gently on the runway

The Bank of China building in the heart of Central District
(Rick Browne).

and roll out toward the sea as the grand panorama of Hong Kong unfolds left and right. Newcomers gasp as they see what must be one of the most singular and remarkable of urban views anywhere.

one would imagine that perhaps only once every few months or so would a person of questionable sanity actually buy such a bottle. But in Hong Kong, the sommelier of this restaurant—who came from

Then there is swift return to the prosaic. The captain snaps open the equalizer valves to bring the cabin pressure back up to normal. Air—it would be idle to call it "fresh air"—promptly floods into the cabin, bringing with it the unforgettably unpleasant smell from the chemical-laden channel alongside the runway, which is known as—and is notorious as—the Kai Tak Nullah. Invariably a newcomer aboard will wrinkle his nose and ask what on earth is causing that terrible reek, allowing some wag to repeat the oldest saw in the book, saying for the umpteenth time, why that, dear fellow, is *the smell of money.*

THE MONEYED FEW in Hong Kong are moneyed beyond reasonable belief. A certain restaurant in the Central District has on its list a selection of vintage Bordeaux that range in price from $1,000 to $5,000 per bottle. In any normal city

France and thus had reason to be incredulous—reported in the papers that he sold five bottles each week, every one of them to his Chinese guests. He reported that they were generally young men, they drove Rolls Royces (of which there are nine hundred in the colony, the most per capita in the world; there are also seventy Bentleys), and they lived in large houses out at Sai Kung or even on The Peak (from which the colonial masters had banned all Chinese residents until 1904). They were possessed of such immense and recently acquired fortunes that even if the Bordeaux cost $50,000 a bottle, they would still buy—because to do so at table, before a gathering of their friends, would give them such an enormous amount of that most supremely important of commodities, Face . . .

The wine list at the Mandarin Grill is good, as befits a place of heavy brass and billows of snowy linen and tanks of slow-swimming tropi-

Foyer of the Peninsula Hotel (James Marshall).

cal fish beside the murals, and it occasionally sports clarets with similarly stratospheric prices. But the sommelier there rarely has the opportunity to present them. Most of his clientele are Western visitors to Hong Kong, and very few of them now have sufficient disposable funds (or perhaps such an all-encompassing desire to gain face) to buy such wine. They come to the Mandarin Grill in legions, however, to deal in a commodity that cannot wholly be equated with money—and that is power.

There are other great hotels in Hong Kong, of course—the Regent, the Shangri-La, the Hilton, and the indefatigable old Peninsula, the Pen—but the most powerful of the colony's power dining places remains the Mandarin. Grill—for power breakfasts any time after seven or, attracting even greater numbers, for power lunches after half past twelve. At these times the Grill sees as discreet a display and interchange of power and influence—colonial satrap breaking bread with monarch's acolyte, senior banker consummating deals with visiting corporate client, senior diplomat finessing policy with senior diplomat—as one is likely to find in the capitalist world.

The same was once true of the Hong Kong Club, just across the square on the far side of the Cenotaph (where a British soldier will have raised the flag and sounded reveille at eight o'clock). But ever since the club had its splendid premises torn down in 1982 and replaced with one of the most undistinguished and unloved pieces of cigarette-box architecture in town, it has lost some of its pull. True, all the taipans are members of the club, and they regularly take tables. But the place has an undeniable air of provincialism about it, its members talking the language of town councilmen and aldermen. The Mandarin Grill, by contrast, is still a place with worldly reach, where the global deals are struck.

(The new club may be ugly, but it is far from being the ugliest building in town. That singular honor goes to the Cultural Centre, built in 1988, a vile and faceless blot that has been compared to a cigarette box that someone has stamped on. It is so dreadful that its architect, a Mr. Jose Lei, rarely admits his responsibility for it.)

GOVERNMENT officially begins its work at nine, as do

The Island Shangri-La, from a window of the Hotel Conrad
(Jodi Cobb).

most of the major companies and the *hongs*, the trading houses. This word, it should be noted, has nothing at all to do with the *Hong* that appears in Hong Kong, which is in any case pronounced *heung* in Cantonese and means "fragrant." The whole meaning of Hong Kong— or Xianggang, as the Mandarin-speaking Chinese plan to rename it— is "fragrant harbor." To anyone recalling the smell of the Kai Tak Nullah on a hot summer's day, this is a somewhat alarming piece of misdescription.

The other *hong*, meaning trading house, is a part of the small vocabulary of strange Chinese-Portuguese-Indian words, themselves reflective of the curious ethnic mix of South China, picked up in short order by anyone who lives here. First there is the word *pidgin*, which comes from the way the Chinese tried to pronounce the word *business* and means that halfway lingo used by traders who can't speak each other's language, and which is memorialized in all those films of the forties and fifties in which people would say things like "So solly, I

thinkee you mean go chop-chop, I makee big mistake for you, boss." There is *comprador*, a word signifying a businessman's middle-man, someone hired for the specific purpose of mediating between the commercial demands of the Chinese and the Westerner. There is *cumshaw*, pidgin for what in countries a little farther west is called baksheesh and which even farther west is called a tip. There is *junk*, actually a Malay word, which describes the rig or the style of hull of the boats on which many a weekend party is now held in the colony. There is *shroff*, originally simply an Urdu term for the man who handles the money, but now refers simply to the car-park attendant who handles the cash. And there is the omnipresent *amah*, the domestic helper, the key to no small measure of the colony's success.

The government of Hong Kong is very large. (In Britain there is one civil servant— including members of the armed forces—for about every 90 members of the population. But in Hong Kong there are 190,000 civil servants, which works out to one for every 30 of the

A judge in robes at Roman Catholic Cathedral ceremony on Hong Kong's Caine Road (Neil Farrin).

inhabitants and which thus renders the bureaucracy proportionately about three times as big.) It has a reputation for being rather fussy and strict, and it plays a rather larger part in the lives of most people in the territory than one would expect given that such tenets as "laissez-faire" and "positive non-interventionism" and concepts such as "a total lack of interference from the government" are usually advanced—by the self-same government—to explain the territory's astonishing success.

This matter of the government's lack of interference is in fact generally limited to its absence from every citizen's right to attempt to make money honestly—an ambition that can fairly be said to be central to life in Hong Kong. It is very little of an exaggeration to say that here, uniquely in the world, you actually can have an idea at breakfast time, set up a company to implement the idea by lunch, and be making money (or losing it) by dinner. The government makes it very easy to do such a thing, and it takes very little away in taxes (no more than 15 percent of personal income, with a man permitted until 1971 to claim a deduction—this being a part of China, after all—for a concubine).

In many other aspects of life, however, this elephantine government works like a Fury to maintain order and primness among its people. It noses around in areas in which more sophisticated democracies have long since abandoned their interest. The practice of homosexuality, for example, was until July 1991 forbidden under a local version of the law that sent Oscar Wilde to prison. Using a megaphone in public places is not permitted, and a group of protesters was fined in 1990 for doing so. An anticorruption unit, set up in the 1970s after the police force was found to be riddled with practitioners of nefarious goings-on—may arrest anyone it likes without a publicly stated reason and hold him for days without any right of appeal to anyone. The showing of a female nipple or more on the cover of a magazine is strictly outlawed. Indeed, there is a committee, the Obscene Articles Tribunal, that, with the help of a pool of "lay assessors,"

*A Chai Wan cemetery during the annual
Ching Ming festival honoring the dead (Rick Browne).*

vets all such material and each week publishes, in explicit detail, its rulings. (Connoisseurs say the details of the orders for affixing tape here, and cutting out that anatomical detail there are probably rather more erotic than the journal they seek to thus sanitize.)

From base to apex, the Hong Kong government—staffed overwhelmingly with Chinese, but with a few thousand Britons, most of whom would fare less well back home but who have pleasing "compensation packages" that, in some well-publicized cases, include passage back to England aboard an ocean liner—manages to keep the place essentially in check. The vastness of the government makes for the official acquisition of all manner of arcane skills. Hong Kong would presumably not be the place it is without the services of, among others, a Cremations Booking Officer, a Senior Passive Amenities Officer, the In-charge of the Goods Seized from Hawkers Store, a Police Centralised Mess Utensils Officer, or an Assistant Director, Squatter Control—the last having as part of his brief a profound hope that all those elderly men and women who visit their dawn-watching gardens each day at four should have emerged from flats on government housing estates and not from huts made of reinforced cardboard and corrugated tin.

Nor would Hong Kong be the same without the man at the summit of this vast mass of bureaucracy, His Excellency the Governor.

The very concept of colonial governorship has vanished from most of the world, as have all empires and most colonies. Portugal has one governor in one colony (Macau, next door to Hong Kong across the Pearl River Estuary, and dignified by being the oldest extant imperial relic in the world). France retains a scattering of its *territoires-outre-mer,* and a somewhat larger number of similar *départements,* which are legally regarded as parts of France. Britain, though, clings steadfastly—or, as it insists, is forced by circumstances to cling steadfastly—to no fewer than sixteen real and copper-bottomed colonies, by far the largest number of all.

To run this far-flung mess of skerries and peninsulas upon which the sun, it is still quite true to say, never does quite set (though it will when in due course Hong Kong reverts to Chinese control), Britain maintains no fewer than eleven colonial governors. All are elegant figures when in full fig, the ceremonial uniform of white drill, with buckskin boots, a sword, and a tall hat plumed with the tail feathers of a goose. But they are, in most cases and in many other senses, rather sorry figures of diplomacy, men who could never lay claim to being in the vanguard of their craft, who have essentially been pensioned off to a place where they can do little harm. What diplomat, for instance, would really wish to end a career that might have culminated in Washington or Paris as governor of such politically forgettable (though physically delightful) places as Saint Helena or Bermuda or to have as the summit of ambition residence in Government House at Plymouth, Montserrat?

Similarly dismissive remarks have been made about the choicest remaining post in the Empire, the governorship of Hong Kong. "On the whole, not much more difficult than being Lord Mayor of Portsmouth," scoffed one of the holders of the post (there have been twenty-seven, the first in 1843). A former British prime minister, James Callaghan, supposedly once offered the job to a colleague while standing occupied with other business in the House of Commons men's room.

It is a job, however, with perks that are as impressive as its powers—powers that are, in essence, absolute. Some say, facetiously but not entirely unfairly, that the governor of Hong Kong presides over the last true dictatorship in Asia, a place where his word is, essentially, law. Of course Kim Il Sung's North Korea is much less democratic than Hong Kong; and in any case, since September 1991, Hong Kong has been allowed to enjoy a vague taste of democracy, with a small proportion of its tiny legislature now actually elected by the people whom it claims to represent. But unlike so many of her other imperial possessions, Britain chose never to offer much by way of political freedom to Hong Kong—not even now, as it tiptoes toward the cold realities of takeover.

Critics have wondered why Britain has offered so little political freedom to the colony, so late. The blunt answer appears to be that the Chinese Communists who take power in 1997 have repeatedly indicated to successive supine

British governments that it would be so much more *convenient* to assume control of a population that, like its own people, was both nicely neutered and politically quiescent. These same Communists have made it clear that they would also prefer that the British, in the closing years of their rule, not give this same Hong Kong citizenry any ideas of democracy that could one day provoke, how shall we say, *tiresome* problems—demonstrations, perhaps, or demands for freedom—that might trouble the rulers-in-waiting. And the British, in what history will surely judge to have been a rather greasy and evasive manner, agreed to do just that—to offer just a sniff of democracy to the Hong Kong people, in order to satisfy public opinion and world opinion; but at the same time to offer nothing of substance to them—nothing that might offend the mainland Chinese. How convenient for all concerned that, though in terms of communist dogma, a British colonial governor is surely anathema, it is undeniable that the power he wields, as well as the machinery with which he does so, presents a most convenient model for a totalitarian regime to copy and assume, intact, without any need for modification. All that the British have to do in the remaining years—despite what the Hong Kong citizenry themselves might want—is nothing.

The colonial governor, appointed to be the messenger for such a policy as this, presides over all in conditions of great physical comfort. He presently has a moderately fine palace in which to live, although it was not regarded as such during World War II when Hong Kong was occupied by the Japanese and thus had a Japanese governor. The most notable of these — and the one who was most critical of the existing Government House — was the first, a certain Rensuke Isogai. He was by all accounts a most unpleasant man but is nonetheless still occasionally mentioned by some of today's older Hong Kong taxi drivers in the same breath as such governors as Sir Hercules Robinson or Sir Alexander Grantham, suggesting that, in some of the more traditional Chinese circles, any authority figure merits respect, be he from London or Tokyo.

Governor Isogai decided that the king's representative whom he had forcibly replaced had lived in accommodations that were less than suitable for the envoy of the Emperor of All-Nippon. He promptly ordered all manner of architectural "improvements," including the installation of sliding doors and shoji screens and tatami mats and today's most visible relic, a tower, eighty feet high, with upturned eaves, that makes the place look like a railway station. The similarity is hardly surprising, since the man that Isogai-san brought in to perform the work was the chief architect of the South Manchurian Railway, who modeled Hong Kong Government House after the station up in Mukden.

This small infelicity of aspect aside, the present governor occupies his position, as have his predecessors, in great style. There is a pleasing summer house conveniently near the Royal Hong Kong Golf Club at Fan Ling, in the New Territories. There is a yacht named the *Lady Maurine.* As commander-in-chief, he can call up a helicopter at a moment's notice. There is a salary approaching that paid to the president of the United States (his Foreign Office salary, moreover, continues to be paid during his posting to this distant colony), a very handsome entertainment allowance, any number of colorful uniforms, ranging from that for the commander-in-chief of British forces to chancellor of the University of Hong Kong. Plus there is a staff of around sixty, from gardeners to private detectives, drivers (of, among other things, the only Rolls Royce Phantom Five allowed to any foreign office diplomat anywhere), and social secretaries.

Indeed, a photograph that might be taken of a governor of Hong Kong in the 1990s, attended by his staff in front of Government House (though such a picture has never been permitted), would not look so very different from that of a viceroy of India taken in the 1930s. The governor, no matter that his colony lives both on the cusp of the twenty-first century and, more important, on the verge of its own colonial extinction, still appears to be a very imperial beast indeed.

His daily calendar, and that of his consort, will be filled with matters of both circumstance and pomp. On an average day, he might be presenting diplomas at schools, handing out awards for environmental concern, meeting heads of parliamentary delegations from Canada and Canton (but as of 1991 not from Russia: the governor's political adviser and his security branch are still, in spite of the events of 1991, advising extreme caution in any dealings with the Soviet Union, even now—a policy that was and still is essentially based on second-guessing Beijing and its possible reaction). The colony's First Lady, on the other hand, might be seeing a deputation of Girl Guides, lunching with one of the many charities of which she is titular head (and thereby supporting a variety of hospitals, animal protection lobbies, homes for the elderly, funds for distressed gentlefolk, and so forth), addressing a group of senior citizens over tea, or talking about the azaleas (for which Government House is renowned) to a gardening club up on The Peak.

Perhaps the most important weekly entry in the governor's diary is the Tuesday morning meeting of the Executive Council, the colony's chief policy-making body. Like the supreme policy-making bodies of all of Britain's earlier and remaining colonies, it meets secretly. It has never been photographed in session. One might, in defense of the institution, mention that much the same degree of secrecy surrounds Britain's equivalent body in London, the Cabinet (though in fact this has been photographed from time to time), with the single rather notable exception that, while in Britain members of the Cabinet are

usually elected into Parliament by the people, in Hong Kong not a single member of Exco, as the body is called, has any popular sanction. Every single member is there either because he or she was appointed by the governor or because the nature of his or her job confers the position.

So, the major general who commands the two thousand British (and four thousand mercenary Nepalese Gurkha) forces in Hong Kong sits on the council. So does the colony's chief secretary, whoever he may be. So does the financial secretary and the attorney general. And then there is a clutch of eleven colonial notables, representing, in the governor's view, various strands of knowledge, opinion, and wisdom.

The chairman of the Hongkong Bank is always there, for instance. There is often a representative of the trading company John Swire & Company, which has such massive investments in the colony (including the modestly sized, highly successful airline Cathay Pacific). These days there is an academic, the vice-chancellor of Hong Kong University. And there are others, of equal stature and note. At their Tuesday meetings, they essentially advise the governor on how he might best run his domain and outline the laws that are sent down to be inevitably approved by the Legislative Council, a body that, almost similarly unrepresentative of the people, sits each Wednesday after lunch.

Were skeptics ever to suggest that the colony is thus run for the primary benefit of such companies as the Hongkong Bank and Messrs.

Swire (who also have member-representatives in the lower house, in common with the other great trading houses of Jardine and Inchcape), they would be energetically shouted down. But it remains a puzzlement to some outsiders that the laws of any city-state in today's world can essentially still be formulated by the companies that have the biggest stake in the place, rather than by the citizenry who live there. It is as though the people of Cincinnati were disenfran-

chised and the government of the city given over to represen-tatives of South-ern Ohio Savings & Loan and Procter & Gam-ble. In Hong Kong, despite a maturation of 150 imperial years, one barely hears a whisper of protest.

THE BANKS, the stock exchange, the futures ex-change, stockbrokerages, and most of the other demonstrable engine-works of capitalism are all open and thundering away by half-past nine. ("It's got to be stopped, it's got to be stopped," a young Briton told Edward Heath at a party in the colony some years ago, prompting the former prime minister to inquire as to just what had to be

stopped. "All this money-making has got to be stopped. It's not healthy for them. They mustn't be allowed to go on running things this way.")

Technology has made the financial institu-tions all outwardly rather bloodless places now, the blinking of electronic lamps having taken the place of the screaming of dealers, the passing of endless streams of liquid crystal digits replacing the ticker and its tape. And though once bankers in silk top hats rushed across town in rickshaws and sedan chairs, that era is long gone: the bankers of Hong Kong are as gray and sedate as any on Wall Street or Cheapside.

But their banks and mar-kets can still be dramatically volatile, and for those with their money hidden under mattresses or in safe havens many miles away, they can provide great entertainment, with scandals aplenty and mismanagement rife. Few in the col-ony will forget the distinguished chairman of the stock exchange ("This is a town where you can make your money—and keep it," was his best-known adage) flying into a televised rage at a reporter who had dared to ask why he had closed the local exchange during the 1987 global

Indoor mall in Kowloon
(Alex Webb).

markets crisis. Was it, the reporter wondered, to help stave off his friends' potential losses? The distinguished chairman looked as though he had been stung by a hornet. He waved his fist. He foamed at the mouth. He threatened all manner of lawsuits. And then he was arrested; he presently languishes in prison, essentially for having bailed out his friends, just as had been alleged.

Then again, Hong Kong is one of those rare towns in which it is actually possible to witness a bank run. Gossip and rumor play a central and perhaps not always unwelcome role in the conduct of business here. (A rumor that the Chinese potentate Deng Xiaoping has died seems to sweep the colony's markets about once every six weeks and usually seems to be followed by a sudden decline in stock prices. One has to wonder, Hong Kong being the kind of place it is, whether these morbid rumors aren't initiated by a broker who is selling short, as they say, and who is thus able to make a modest killing every time the market reacts to such news by spiraling downward briefly.)

But while stock markets everywhere are afflicted and affected by rumors, banks in other parts of the world customarily remain aloof. Not so in Hong Kong. There is a nervousness, a jitteriness, a skittishness about the territory that makes it at once an exciting and dangerous place in which both to make money and, as the former stock market chairman said, to keep it. Rumors cannonade from one end of Victoria to another in seconds, often producing remarkable results.

Not too long ago a chain of cake stores, Maria's, introduced gift certificates, usually for 15 Hong Kong dollars (about US$2: the rate has for the past decade been fixed at HK$7.80 to US$1), which were immediately traded as scrip. But then, for some unaccountable reason, a rumor swept the colony that Maria's was in some sort of trouble. With impressive speed hundreds of thousands of Hong Kongers (by which unlovely name the citizenry is now generally known) found their cake certificates and rushed to the nearest store to exchange them for cakes. Lines formed along entire city blocks, and old men and women were seen staggering away under piles of Rich Dundee and Chocolate Bundt and Cherry Cream Slice that they presumably had

A poster announces a new Jackie Chan movie
at the corner of Nathan Road and Jordan Road in Kowloon (Alex Webb).

neither the time nor the appetite to consume. Maria's survived (no word, however, on some of her carbohydrate-laden customers), and so, uniquely, did the phenomenon of mass financial hysteria that briefly afflicted her.

As with the shops, so with some of the colony's banks. For example, Citibank, an establishment not exactly known for its lack of willingness to meet its obligations, was hit by a run in mid-1991. The London-based bank Standard Chartered, which is not always in the best of health but which still had coffers full of cash, was hit a few days later. Suggestions that they might have what are charmingly known as "liquidity problems" swept the territory one morning; by lunchtime long lines could be seen outside the banks' offices, with policemen and security guards (the latter usually Indians, sons of the Indians who used to police the International Settlement in Shanghai) trying gamely to keep order.

The parallel with Shanghai is beguiling. The image that comes to mind each time such an episode is witnessed in Hong Kong is that captured on film by Henri Cartier-Bresson and his Leica in 1948, with a frantic, panicky scramble of Chinese trying desperately to convert their paper money into gold before the Communists took over. And while that was never the motivating force behind the panics and the runs at Chartered or Citibank or the infamous BCCI during the same year, the symbolism was apt: banks in a colony nearing the end of its colonial existence do not necessarily seem quite as safe to investors as they should. Not, at least, to the preternaturally cautious and ever suspicious Chinese.

Gold is still much favored by these most financially circumspect of people. True, once he has made it, once he is truly rich, the Hong Kong Chinese will spend his money with unrivaled abandon—the buying of Petrus Bordeaux or the finest of brandies or the most costly of cars will continue unabated through recession, depression, collapse, and chaos. But while the Hong Kong Chinese is making his money—when he is at his most impressive, his most (to the awestruck Westerner) daunting—he will work and save and be more astute and financially cunning than almost anyone imaginable.

At this stage, every chance for a profit is taken, every opportunity for saving is exploited. Margins are shaved to the bone; savings are checked by the day; market prices and exchange rates are scrutinized by the hour. Many a luncheon or cocktail party (an institution of which Hong Kong is peculiarly fond) is suddenly interrupted by the buzz of a dozen electronic beepers that have automatically alerted holders of *this* stock or *that* currency that *now* is the moment to sell or *now* is the time to buy.

It is for this man, the man on the lower rungs of the ladder, that the Royal Observatory's time signal (broadcast every half-hour, a peculiarity of Hong Kong) is most important, for not a few young Chinese need to know, or claim to need to know, the position of their holdings or their stakes or their portfolios every few *minutes* during a particularly dramatic financial day, so that they can issue instructions (via cellular telephones, of course—there are more of these here, per capita, than anywhere else on earth) to buy or sell or whatever, in the hope of making or saving those few extra dollars or few hundred thousand dollars, to give them a better chance, a better future, an opportunity to pull themselves up and into the light.

It should be remembered that for most of the six million people in Hong Kong, the colony exists solely to offer them an opportunity for personal betterment. Nearly all of the population, which is overwhelmingly Chinese (fewer than 250,000 are the *gweilos*, the white ghosts, the long-noses, the barbarian foreigners, the non-Chinese) have, one or two generations back, lived in conditions of quite abject poverty. Most of them are from China's Guangdong province, though a few are Hokkienese, a few are Shanghainese, and rather more are Hakkas, the so-called "guest people" or southern Chinese gypsies, and most of them fled to Hong Kong and to British protection and sanctuary after the Chinese communist revolution of 1949.

When they arrived—and many tell the most heartrending tales of their passage here, swimming or running or walking for days, dodging guards and wire and dogs, with the prospect of the most severe punishment from their own side if captured en route—most of the migrants were in the pathetic condition of most refugees. They were poor, destitute, hungry. Yet they were not at all hopeless. They were, instead, to everyone's admiration, extraordinarily ambitious, and more than willing, if given a chance, to work unbelievably hard, to spend frugally, to save strictly, to haul themselves up by their frayed bootstraps. What China's province of Guangdong could never, under its political and economic system, have offered them the opportunity to do, Hong Kong could. And many—most, one can say with confidence—promptly succeeded in so bettering themselves, most within the span of a generation, or less.

There is, consequently, a fierceness, a defiance, in all these people's desires for self-improvement. Many Westerners come to Hong Kong and deride it for its materialism, for its all-too-obvious displays of avarice and vulgarity, for its ostentation, for its obsession with money-making. But perhaps such a critic should pause for a moment and consider: if you yourself were dirt-poor and had no future, and you came across a place not far from home to which it was possible, though difficult, to flee, where the rules allowed you to exploit your talents and to realize your ambitions and to lift yourself up from such poverty as you had known, a place guaranteeing—if not for you, then for your children and your grandchildren—a life as good as the very best you have ever heard about, would you not strive for it too? Moreover, would you not make use of your time in this extraordinary place to ensure that poverty was a word that could never again be applied to you, one that vanished from your personal lexicon?

This is exactly the case for the great majority of the people who now populate Hong Kong. A powerful collective memory—of former poverty, of running away, of breaking into a new society, of making a new life in a hurry—all of this, lurking somewhere just beneath the surface of every Chinese mind, helps to sustain a profound racial division between the Hong Kong Chinese and those of other origins. It is a division that is more serious than it looks, one that keeps each side from understanding the other fully. It blights Hong Kong in a way that, say, Singapore has never been blighted. And at the heart of the misunderstanding is the assumption among many Westerners in Hong Kong that the desire for self-improvement among the Chinese is nothing more than greed and that the Chinese are—one hears the remark almost every day—*only interested in money.* It is not nearly so simple. What drives the Hong Kongers to work so hard, to make their fortunes with such mind-boggling rapidity, is linked in part to that powerful collective memory, the ever-present specter of how life could have been for them but, mercifully, never was. What so many are tempted to call greed is actually no more and no less than ambition, laudable and admirable ambition, writ large and performed at breakneck speed. Would that more nations had such energy—would there be so many Bangladeshes and Malis

and Madagascars if collective memory and zeal and energy were as magically fused there as they apparently are in Hong Kong?

AT NOON EACH DAY, a small reminder of empire sounds over the colony. It comes from a small naval gun mounted on a concrete plinth by the shore of Causeway Bay, a pretty little Victorian brassbound cannon, the kind used to start yacht races and, well, to sound noonday guns. This particular gun, part talisman, part tourist attraction, is in the care of an employee of Jardine, Matheson & Company, perhaps the best known (at least to readers of James Clavell) of the great hongs of Hong Kong.

The firing—which is as accurate as the final pip of the six sent out from the observatory, if only because that is where the gun's keeper gets his time, from a small radio pressed to his ear—is a relic of a good-humored penalty imposed on the company by the Royal Navy, which was reportedly vexed when one of the Jardine's taipans was welcomed back to his territory with a multigun salute, an honor that should have been reserved for welcoming back the governor or the commander of the fleet. It is also a daily reminder of the firm's unlovely history—and of its intimate connections with the unlovely beginnings of Hong Kong's own story.

It is all rather less distinguished than so pretty a ceremony as the noonday gun suggests. Jardine's originally was no more than a company of Scottish grocers. In the early part of the last century, they were making small fortunes in the Orient by transporting cakes of Patna opium across to China and thereby feeding a popular addiction to the drug among the ordinary Chinese. It was a trade about which the Chinese government, not surprisingly, at first felt uneasy and then wholly opposed.

But China's opposition was not taken kindly. It was seen by the imperial-minded government in London, backers of Jardine's commerce and profitability, who somehow conflated this mercantile notion into the more general theories of commerce and principles of free trade and so forth—as damaging to British commercial interests and rights. Powerful warships were accordingly sent to defend the empire's dignity. The Chinese, who were woefully ill prepared, utterly lacking in any kind of war-making technology, and weakened by myriad internal schisms, lost the ensuing war. And in 1841, the island of Hong Kong was handed over to Queen Victoria in perpetuity, as part of the spoils of the sorry little episode.

It is perhaps small wonder that China, a century and a half later, should still feel a sense of embitterment, that so ugly a trade and so unequal a war should have led to the granting of eternal rights to foreigners—from whom China has in any case long felt culturally alienated—to possess a valuable piece of southern Chinese territory. Many British, however, see neither injustice nor irony in the situation, even now.

One still hears, in London and Hong Kong, more than a little evidence of a wholesale lack of sympathy with the view that China might properly wish to possess all of China and wish to purge itself of all foreign tenants. Instead, the holders of such views like to utter such Latinisms as *si monumentum requiris, circumspice;* they like to note that Jardine's is now one of the world's grandest and richest and most successful companies, and Hong Kong, one of the world's grandest and richest and most successful territories. They argue that China derives much benefit from the very existence of the Hong Kong that Britain helped create, and so why are the Chinese grumbling about it anyway?

THE SOUNDING OF THE CANNON coincides with the appearance on the Hong Kong scene of a hitherto somnolent part of society, the *tai-tais.* Middle-aged, Chinese, formidable, well dressed,

The Yip family share a family dinner in their jade shop (Basil Pao).

and rich, these married women with the luxury of both time and money on their hands (Ladies who Lunch, the phrase might well translate to, though in fact it comprises all married Chinese women) descend from their houses and flats on The Peak and the South Side and the Mid-Levels to a warren of private rooms in the myriad Chinese restaurants around Central and Wanchai and Causeway Bay to eat *dim sum*, to chatter at enormous volume, and perhaps, to while away their afternoons playing cards or else the game that the American Joseph Babcock named (and copyrighted) Mah-Jongg, which in Hong Kong is called *ma cheuk*. The ladies tend to play a genteel version, at a volume appropriate to their social station; but when men play, especially when they do so illicitly for money, the noise of clattering plastic tiles and the raucous shouts of *pung!* and *chow!* surely render this the noisiest game on earth, producing one of the most unmistakable sounds that form a bass *continuo* to life in today's Hong Kong.

Hong Kong's lunch hour is a sacred institution. At one level it provides a scale for rating the current eco-nomic health of the colony (the Mandarin Grill can serve 120 luncheons, and it is reckoned that if all tables are full, the territory is in good shape; if less than a hundred turn up, the economy is in deep depression). At the other it can display the sheer speed at which steamed buns and bowls of rice and chickens' feet and fried frogs and braised duck and minced pigeon can be prepared and served and fed to customers at restaurants so large as to accommodate two thousand diners at a single sitting. The Chinese are, despite their stature and frame, prodigious eaters, fascinated with and fastidious about their diets and the yin and yang of the various plates put before them. "How are you today?" we ask in the West. "Have you had your rice yet?" is the afternoon salutation of the Hong Kong Chinese.

AFTER LUNCH the territory appears to still. A suburban hush seems to fall upon the streets, shutters are pulled down against the heat, and people strive to keep out of the direct sun, which glares angrily down from a brassy sky. Up in the hills and out

Egg vendor on Apliu Street in Sham Shui Po, in Kowloon (Robert Maass).

on the water, cooler routines continue. The ferries still scuttle to and fro across the harbor. The shadow of the world's biggest Buddha lengthens out at the Lantau monastery, and his attendant priests up among the tea plantations intone their sacred liturgies. The British and Nepali soldiers—there has been another shift change in the afternoon—still patrol the frontier.

The little British naval vessels chuckle around the faraway islands, exercising and teaching midshipmen the finer points of navigation. The Royal Marines, burly men in lithe little rubber boats, give chase to smugglers who try to sneak cargoes of television sets or motorcars (which are sometimes towed underwater, sealed entirely in huge black rubber balloons, like car-carrying condoms) out to China.

While British Marines are trying to help prevent goods from leaving illicitly, the Hong Kong marine police at the same time are usually to be found welcoming and then promptly detaining (after delousing) that day's wretched collection of refugees who have arrived in territorial waters after sailing their leaky little boats

three hundred miles, from the coast of Vietnam. The refugees, tens of thousands of them now, are held after processing, like so many cattle, in special camps. They are treated like prisoners, held behind wire, with few privileges and fewer rights, until a panel of judges decides, each case one at a time, whether the would-be immigrant has fled to this island of wealth and comparative freedom for economic or political reasons.

If the judges decide he has come in search of prosperity, then his knuckles are rapped and he is sent to a specially secure camp, to await the day he can be returned to Vietnam, by force, if need be. If, on the other hand, the panel believes his assertion that he came to escape political persecution (a rarity: perhaps one in twelve is believed), he is classified as a real refugee, is given much more pleasing quarters, and is told to wait—in some cases for many years—until another country will accept him as an immigrant.

But because geography and tide and wind and season dictate that most refugees who turn up in Hong Kong come from what was once

The cubicles of asylum-seekers at the
High Island Detention Center (Leong Ka Tai).

North Vietnam, and because the United States, which has the room to accept most Vietnamese refugees, is generally disinclined to accept men and women from the north, most of those who end up in Hong Kong stay there, in execrable conditions, for a long, long time.

Small armies of volunteers, most of them foreigners, visit the huge camps, trying to make their stay a little easier and to teach them English or the violin or some skill that might eventually be of use. The Chinese stay at a distance, regarding the Vietnamese with disdain and worse. There was a terrible battle in the late 1980s when it was decided that Vietnamese refugee children might be allowed to study at a Chinese school: racial prejudice—and often a much more profound degree of separation divides some kinds of Asians than does the initially more obvious gulf between Asians and Westerners—is an ugly feature of life in many parts of China. It seems all the uglier when it occurs in so prosperous and fortunate a quarter as Hong Kong.

For most of those who come, there is precious little hope of ever securing a home in another country. And yet, courageous or foolhardy, they still arrive, scores each day when the winds are in the right direction. Hong Kong each day thus becomes still more swamped by the tide of immigrants. The colony's budgets for housing and feeding them become ever more strained. Tensions—among those who guard the refugees, among the refugees themselves, between groups originally from the north and from the south, between those held in the camps for years and those who are newcomers—become acute. Tempers are stretched to the limit. Fights break out. There are riots, outbreaks of arson and mayhem, occasional murders. It is an unhappy situation, one in which few in the colony, other than the tireless legions of volunteers, can take much pride.

As the sun begins to dip and the heat begins to wane, so the streets start to fill once more. Schoolchildren, their backs bowed under burdens of schoolbooks (in 1986 a survey showed a dismayingly large number of local children suffered spinal damage from carrying such heavy satchels), creep back to their homes and to their homework (or to help in the family restaurant or flower shop or around the house, or to read to grandmother or do whatever chore falls to the youngest in that tight little mutual, multigenerational support system that is a Chinese family). Chinese *amahs*, their backs similarly bowed by decades of scrubbing floors and sewing hems, chatter while waiting for elevators. Filipina domestic helpers—they say they dislike the use of the Chinese word *amah*—walk dogs or bring home small infants from daycare or the park.

There are some 73,000 Philippine nationals in Hong Kong, the largest of the various troupes of foreign workers. Most are women, doing domestic work, and very few are content working as they do. Their presence here is another of the unsung oddities of Hong Kong, another small reason for the success of the place, yet a dismaying testimony to the lack of success of a neighbor-nation less than a two-day sail away (close enough for the Royal Hong Kong Yacht Club to organize weekend races, during which such tedious topics as the comparative economies of the neighbors are never mentioned).

The Philippines is a country currently in a dreadful state. Its economy is half-ruined, its spirit broken, its cities worn out and decayed. Few of its people can get work that offers much beyond a living wage. But Hong Kong, sixty minutes away on a Philippines Airlines jet, offers work in abundance—provided that the potential worker will do as he or she is bidden, regardless of what his or her qualifications happen to be.

The result of this inequity is that Hong Kong now teems with young women—irrepressibly cheerful and enthusiastic young women—who may well have university degrees or diplomas in this or that from colleges and technical institutes from Luzon to Zamboanga but work in Hong Kong cleaning other people's houses and washing other people's clothes and feeding other people's children. Such degradation—and almost all of the women admit privately that what they do does degrade them and all too often drives them to despair—is the only means, sad to say, by which these women can afford to clothe, feed, and educate the children—too many children, in that most Catholic of countries—that they have been forced to leave behind.

So all the better apartments in Hong Kong are designed with special rooms—*amah*'s quarters, the real estate offices call them, as if they were barracks—in which the maids live during their off-hours. The rooms are usually mean, with no air conditioning, a bath so small as to suggest the user is somehow smaller than the rest of humanity, and none of the luxuries enjoyed by the apartment's owners beyond the kitchen door (which is equipped with a small window so the maid can see exactly when the next course needs serving and need not disturb the household with her presence).

And while many employers treat their *amahs* well—though the official pay scale allows a live-in maid just $400 monthly, about a third of the restaurant price of one of the cheaper bottles of Petrus—a great many do not. Cruelty, abuse, unfair dismissal, the withholding of wages and passports—the complaints of this exploited group of women are legion.

At the same time the very existence, which in Hong Kong is taken for granted, of inexpensive and pliant domestic helpers manages to instill in the mind—particularly in the colonial, expatriate mind—a vision of a way of life that was probably hitherto wholly unfamiliar and is, consequently, perhaps not wholly healthy. A young man comes out to the East to work as a mid-level bureaucrat or banker (and if a bachelor banker, he lives first in an institution called a mess, as though service in Hong Kong was akin to that in the army), and he finds he no longer has to cook or clean his floors or wash his shirts. All is done for him, for the price each month of a decent lunch for two. Small wonder that those returning from Hong Kong some years later are known as "when-I's," for they grumble unceasingly, whining about the weather and the poor service in shops and the fact that one has to scrub one's own collars— it was never like this "when I. . . ."

Evening sees these maids, overworked and underpaid, silhouetted in the kitchens of ten thousand flats, ironing shirts or heating formula or preparing dinners, attending to the duties of a day that has, for them, gone on far too long already. Small wonder that these same maids are the first to

escape to, and the last to leave, the half-tawdry, half-glittering world of the Hong Kong night, one that opens up in Wanchai and extends over the harbor in Tsim Sha Tsui as soon as darkness settles in. If any one group of Hong Kong's citizenry needs friendship and fast music and a few bottles of San Miguel, it is the Filipina maids, uprooted from home, friends only with each other. Or friends with any available man (and one finds that almost every man *mirabile*

dictu, is available) from the USS *Independence* or the USS *Ranger* or the *Blue Ridge,* for the five days of shore leave, or if they're lucky, for their dream of a lifetime of security back in the United States.

HONG KONG NIGHTS have long been safer than nights in most neighboring cities. You don't hear the wail of sirens or the clatter of running feet or the morning-after tales of muggings and shootings that one has heard for years in New York and London and which one hears increasingly in Bangkok and Manila and Djakarta. You live on an outlying island and have to leave a party to catch that midnight hydrofoil? No one would turn a hair if you decided to walk. You can't sleep, and decide to jog at midnight. Few would advise against it. Or at least they wouldn't have until about a year ago.

Since the start of the 1990s, for no credible reason that the Royal Hong Kong Police can suggest, there has been a sudden and disturbing increase in the amount of violent crime. Men committing robberies are using guns of impressive caliber and firepower, all imported from

*A worker stands high on bamboo scaffolding
above Western District (Neil Farrin).*

China. Some gangs have taken to throwing grenades made for the People's Liberation Army at each other and at the police. There are reports of intimidation and threats, of robberies that take place in broad daylight, of protection money demanded under the very noses of detectives.

The infamous Triads—the criminal gangs that have a long and not wholly dishonorable tradition steeped in Chinese politics—seem to be hard at work. The police are apparently incapable of dealing with them, as more and more of the members of the various gangs known to exist in the colony are beginning to act more and more openly, with steadily increasing bravado. Anti-Triad acts, Triad task forces, Triad hotlines: the police try them all, and yet the Triad societies still manage to compete successfully for the loyal membership of tens of thousands—maybe hundreds of thousands—of young Chinese men.

The development has not been wholly unanticipated. A dozen years ago, when it was first rumored that Britain might one day permit China to resume control over her former terri-

tory, some policemen wondered out loud whether the Triad societies would step up their activities, in an attempt to extract as much profit from the colony as possible before the Chinese Communists came in and lowered the boom on their activities. It was assumed that the party ideologues would move swiftly to close nightclubs and massage parlors (known charmingly as "villas" in Hong Kong), would clamp down on illegal gambling (and possibly on legal gambling as well, to the chagrin of the Royal Hong Kong Jockey Club, which sports a pair of billion-dollar racetracks and an income that rivals many nations' GNPs), and would eradicate loansharking and prostitution. The Triads' income from such sources would be swiftly-eliminated.

There would still be plenty of corruption in the territory, another field from which the Triads have profited. In fact there would probably be rather more, since today's China is a nation of institutionalized improbity. But there would be a difference in that the beneficiaries of corruption in tomorrow's Communist-run Hong Kong will be those who benefit from it in today's

A beggar makes his way along a
Causeway Bay sidewalk (Rob Nelson).

Communist China: the middle-ranking cadres in the Communist party—not capitalist-minded gangsters like the Triads. They, for once, would be left very much out in the cold.

So, just as the police expected, an awareness of these dismaying developments forced the Triad leaders to start trying to make their money more quickly, with the ultimate intention of eventually getting both the money, and themselves, out of the colony. The trend began at the end of the 1980s, and it continues apace today. Many of the colony's laws are being broken, and a growing number of people are getting hurt. The police and the army (who would be brought in to help, *in extremis*) are suddenly somewhat alarmed. Law and order in Hong Kong today seems, for the first time in many generations, to have become unusually fragile.

SUCH DISMAL CONCERNS matter little, though, to the colony's buoyant little social set. Night after night during the social season, the same few score of Peak Ladies—a group that overlaps, but is not exclusive to, the *tai-tais* of the *dim sum* and *yum cha* and the afternoon *ma cheuk* sessions—gird themselves up in their ball gowns and proceed to parade themselves in the name of charity, fun, and social mountaineering.

There are any number of charity committees or organizing committees for such institutions as the philharmonic or the ballet, which encourage them to do so. They are invariably staffed by a number of ladies, both formidable

and rich—and both Chinese and *gweipo*—who reputedly fight eagerly to be elected to serve and who then arrange with precision and élan the social calendar of their year in office. Their parties are grand and gaudy. Most have themes—the China Coast, say, or The Fifties or Heaven and Hell. Costume balls are a particular favorite, and masked balls are staged once in a while. All the parties, which are held in the ballrooms of the more opulent hotels (the Grand Hyatt is the current favorite) have handsome price tags. But there is little exclusivity. Anyone may attend: one simply hands over large amounts of cash, buys a table, seats one's friends, and dances the night away.

With good fortune a photographer from a monthly, perhaps *The Peak* or *The Tatler*, will be there, and maybe a writer will conduct a brief and flattering interview. Many a brief social career has been thus launched: Australian ladies seem particularly accomplished in the field. Flash photographs of them, each looking a little tipsy and with a décolletage that is perhaps slightly inappropriate for her age, may be seen in the glossy magazine that few except her friends will read. The caption will be kind: "Repulse Bay's irrepressible Dottie Bunten, in a peach organdy creation of her mother's design, tripping the light fantastic at this year's Liposuction Ball in the Island Shangri-La."

The younger set tends to divide quite neatly in two. The Chinese, bespectacled young men in Hugo Boss suits, who drive BMW Eight Series cars and wear watches by Phillipe Charriol, take their elegant girlfriends to the finer Cantonese restaurants—and there are some, like the redoubtable Fook Lam Moon, where a bowl of gelatinous soup can cost $200 and where it is definitely most chic to be seen. The Westerners, perhaps smooth young cadets from Swire's and Jardine's or Inchcape, are pink-faced, fresh-scrubbed, and ever eager for the sensual pleasures of the East. Seemingly rolled out and snipped off in six-foot lengths of pinstripe, they take their Cathay Pacific stewardesses (known in the local argot as *LBFM*s, little brown fucking machines) to the discotheques and bars scattered around the territory.

If the relationship progresses, then it is weekends in Phuket or Puerto Azul. And if the parental instruction, "Do what you like in the East, but on no account bring it back home" is ignored, then there could well be a wedding (though Swire's once forbade its cadets to marry local girls, and among some British firms' senior echelons, it is still considered rather bad form), with all the attendant delights and complications such a union invariably brings.

AND ALL THE WHILE, far from the buzz of the colony's unstoppable nightlife, the planes rumble up and away from the single runway out at Kai Tak Airport. In early evening the departing traffic is still essentially local—the last Manila flight, the final Seoul, the last two of what could almost be the Taipei Shuttle. But as the night deepens, so the long hauls, the big boys, start their deafening takeoff rolls, thundering off into the dark skies, bound for Europe, America, Australia. All of them are heavy planes, giant Boeings laden with fuel and with cargo—and very heavy with passengers. Hundreds of them are Chinese passengers, many of whom will never return to Hong Kong.

Since the start of the decade, the government's statisticians now reluctantly admit that no fewer than 62,000 people have been leaving the colony, for good, each year. Put more starkly, 170 people fly away each evening with the firm intention of setting up home away from Hong Kong, of living the rest of their lives elsewhere.

By doing so they are uttering a devastating judgment on what they each consider the likely future of the place they have thus far been pleased to call their home. By flying away, to live in Vancouver or Sydney or San Francisco or wherever, they have decided that, in essence, they do not trust the coming of the mainland Chinese. They do not believe what all the smooth and persuasive and skilled diplomats have told them, that everything will be all right, that there will be no change in anyone's style of life, that a solemn and binding agreement between the United Kingdom and the People's Republic, signed by honorable people who have the best interests of the citizenry at heart, positively *guarantees* the immutability of the Hong Kong way of life. "*Fai wa!*" they say instead. "Nonsense! We've heard it all before."

Each one of these 170 passengers who leave for good each night has decided not to accept the blandishments, the seductive assurances, the up-beat editorials. None will believe the optimistic assessments of the geomancers and the stargazers and the temple fortune tellers, whose utterances play so central a role in the life of the average Chinese citizen. Each emigrant has instead taken stock and made a simple calculation.

On all sides there seems to be evidence. Bank runs, refugee riots, the sudden influx of powerful weapons, the growing influence of the Triads—could Hong Kong's social stability be beginning, at long last, to unravel? Is the old place going to remain peaceful, right up until the end? Or will Britain leave behind a half-wrecked city, an urban jungle lost in swirls of tear-gas smoke, with the sound of marching boots crunching over broken glass?

Then again, what of the colony's institutions? The free press that is so treasured—will it be permitted to remain so free? The legal system, so evidently fair and so cherished—could that all change, to the show trial and the kangaroo court and the sudden single bullet in the back of the neck? And what of Hong Kong's vast array of possibilities for self-realization, for self-betterment, for pulling oneself up by the bootstraps—will all this come to an end? Will the Hong Kong of the future come to look and feel like the China of the present?

With the Communists north of the border fence just waiting to take over, it has to be admitted that there is something of a risk that all will go badly awry. Maybe it is a small risk. That, after all, is what the colonial government wishes the citizenry to believe, and it is a view that it takes great pains and expense to promote. Maybe the government is right. Maybe the odds of disaster really are very low indeed.

But then again, this is no hundred-dollar gamble on a horse or a spin of the wheel in the casino at Macau, where the odds do not really matter all that much. This, the emigrant will say, is about *life*—his own (for most primary emigrants are men) and that of his family and that of generations of his family yet unborn. Given the stakes, however minuscule the risk may be, is it worth taking? He weighs it all, he takes stock of what he loves about Hong Kong, he imagines the specter of a nightmare future, and he sets it all against the promises and the predictions. And he answers, eventually and unhesitatingly and unequivocally, *no*. For even with the risk so demonstrably low, the stakes, he considers, are incalculably high.

So he lodges his application—with the Canadian commission or the American consulate or the Australians. He waits, endlessly, as he edges up the list. He is called for interviews, again and again. He stands in line for hours, for days even. He waits, as all Hong Kong people have become well accustomed to doing. And then, finally, he wins the approval. A stamp is stamped in his passport, and he is told he can buy his ticket.

He can call in the packers, he can close his bank accounts and pay his taxes and tell his landlord and quit his job and have a final dinner of Chiu Chow goose and Napoleon brandy and take one last long lingering look at the pretty girls in the bars on Hennessy Road. And then he can board his jet (having ensured himself a good seat in the back, in Smoking) and with a good glass of cognac in his hand and barely a backward glance, he can go, with 169 others beside him, to his new life. He becomes part of that lifeblood of Hong Kong that is draining away so alarmingly fast, while all of those who direct the running of the place—and who tried in vain to convince him to stay—look on, helpless and puzzled.

Maybe one day the hemorrhage will ease. Everything, essentially, depends on China and on the perception that the Hong Kong Chinese have of how their neighbor—their owner-in-waiting—will treat their delicate little city-state. Perhaps, some optimists say, a change will take place in China itself soon, one that will restore some measure of ease and serenity to those who remain and will send out reassuring signals to those who have already gone but might be tempted to return. Perhaps, says almost everyone else. But probably not.

Hong Kong, a hard place, proud of its reputation as tough and merciless, is more frail and perishable an institution than it outwardly appears. After all, the land on which it was built never in the first place belonged to those who built it; it was China's. And the time that is so precisely signaled from the Royal Observatory is time that has essentially been borrowed. For a century and a half, the debt of land and time has been overlooked, ignored, or just forgotten by both sides. But now, at last, China has decided, as she has long had a perfect right to do, to gather in her skirts about her, to make her nation whole. She has accordingly given notice and called the two debts in.

In other circumstances, in other times, and with other countries, this might not present a problem. But given the past and present nature of the nation that is calling in the obligations, one cannot help but be uneasy about the future. Uneasy, anxious, and—for those who have a stake, or a life, in what will soon no longer be Her Majesty's Crown Colony of Hong Kong—even rather frightened.

*Small farms in the New Territories near the Sham Chun,
or Shen Zhen, River (Jodi Cobb).*

HONG

HERE BE DRAGONS

KONG

PHOTOGRAPHS BY

SUSAN BIDDLE

RICK BROWNE

JODI COBB

NEIL FARRIN

LEONG KA TAI

ROBERT MAASS

JAMES MARSHALL

ROB NELSON

BASIL PAO

ELI REED

ALEX WEBB

Feng shui *expert Koon Lung takes a reading from his* lo p'an *compass in Hong Kong's Central District. Hong Kong people look to* feng shui *(wind-water), the ancient Chinese science, to help balance the spiritual and man-made worlds. Its principles determine the placement and design of buildings, and few developers would begin construction without consulting an expert (Robert Maass).*

FACING PAGE:
A worker stands at the base of a bamboo-scaffolded construction site, common in the territory's urban areas. The bamboo scaffolding used to build Hong Kong's high-rises is strong, more resilient than steel, and a renewable resource. It is not particularly safe, however. "Fall of person" ranks as the most common of all the occupational fatalities reported each year in Hong Kong (Robert Maass).

TOP: Traders touch seller in a move seemingly more typical of an athletic field than one of the world's largest gold-trading centers. According to the rules of the Chinese Gold and Silver Exchange Society, the first trader to touch a seller's body gets to make the first offer. It's strictly a male preserve. Women are not permitted to deal (Jodi Cobb). MIDDLE: Office workers arrive at Central MTR (Mass Transit Railway) Station during morning rush hour. Transporting 2.1 million riders daily, the MTR ranks first in the world in passengers per mile (Leong Ka Tai). BOTTOM: The Landmark is one of many upscale indoor malls offering merchandise for sophisticated shoppers (Rick Browne).

■ ■

FACING PAGE: A trader takes a Nintendo break at the Hong Kong Stock Exchange, which was Asia's third-largest stock market in 1990 (Leong Ka Tai).

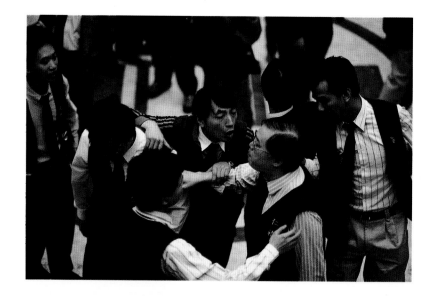

Hong Kong's world-famous hotels, including the Mandarin Oriental, have helped it attract more visitors than anywhere else in Asia. Even after the Tiananmen Square massacre, when a downturn in China tourism hurt Hong Kong, the territory remained first in the region (James Marshall).

■■

PAGES 62 AND 63: A street sweeper cleans up after the predawn distribution of newspapers to vendors in Central District (James Marshall).

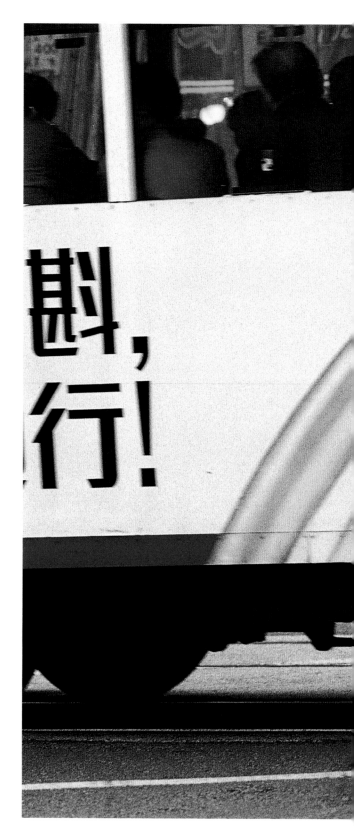

Fourth-generation Hong Kong resident Christine Chao, 37, a respected portraitist, paints her mother's image (Eli Reed).

■■

RIGHT: An elderly gentleman waits for a tram car. Brightly painted trams, which today advertise everything from airlines to analgesic oils, have been traveling the tracks of Hong Kong Island since 1905 and still serve as a major form of public transport (Eli Reed).

CENTRAL DISTRICT

A teenage student from Royden School takes a turn showing off his skateboarding skills in front of a group of friends on the steps leading to the Admiralty MTR Station in Central District. The crowded living conditions endured by many Hong Kong families—often with several generations squeezed into small apartments—force some young people to spend much of their free time outside their homes (Susan Biddle).

Filipina servants, known as amahs, *gather in Statue Square on Sunday, their only day off, to share news, read letters from home, and relax. Although many worked as nurses, teachers, and other professionals in their own country, the minimum monthly wage of HK$3,200 —a special minimum rate for domestic servants—is more than they would make at home and often supports whole families back in the Philippines (Jodi Cobb).*

A bride wears her wedding gown for the brief—about five minutes—and simple ceremony at the marriage registry office. Afterwards, she will change into a traditional Chinese gown to greet the guests at her banquet (Robert Maass).

FACING PAGE:
In their heyday early in this century, hundreds of rickshaw pullers provided the main form of transport in the territory. Today only about 11 rickshaw licenses are issued each year (Rob Nelson).

Hong Kong

A homeless woman guards all her material possessions near the outer-islands-ferry terminal in Central District on Hong Kong Island. The government collects careful statistics on what it calls "active street sleepers." Yau Ma Tei in Kowloon has by far the greatest number of these people, while the outer islands and Tuen Mun usually have none (Basil Pao).

Jane Mackley, an Irish teenager who lives in Hong Kong with her parents, tutors three-year-old Jackie Pun Hing Seng in English. The child began English lessons at the age of two; parents who can afford to do so rigorously prepare their children for life in the global community (Rick Browne).

■■

FACING PAGE:
Kazuo Wada, the owner of the Japanese Yaohan grocery and department store chain, moved its headquarters to Hong Kong in 1989, soon after the Tiananmen incident. The Japanese investment rate in Hong Kong in 1990 exceeded that of the U.S.; analysts say Japanese companies are positioning themselves to move quickly into the potentially huge marketplace of the People's Republic after 1997 (Leong Ka Tai).

■■

PAGES 74 AND 75: Kai-Bong Chao helps his wife, Brenda, into her pink mink. The couple's pink and gold Rolls Royces and their home's unique decor have made them one of Hong Kong's most talked-about couples (Susan Biddle).

TOP: Old-style architecture still predominates in Hong Kong's Western District, though newer architecture has begun to change the look of the neighborhood. The building that houses the Him Tai Hing Kee Company, a dried-food business on Wing Lok Street, is scheduled for demolition because it is structurally unsound. BOTTOM: A traditional Western District tea shop (Both, James Marshall).

■ ■

FACING PAGE: An old-style Western District street (James Marshall).

TOP: Tong Ming Chi, owner of Hung Chong Tai Tea Company, and his employees package 180,000 pounds of tea for export annually. BOTTOM: Rows of pressed ducks imported from China hang in a Western District shop. The ducks are steamed on top of rice as a winter specialty. RIGHT: Western District shop employees hand-mix several varieties of rice together in stainless-steel tubs. The mixtures are then rebagged and sold both wholesale and retail. The men work 12-hour days, six days per week. Hong Kong labor law limits overtime for women workers but not for men (All, James Marshall).

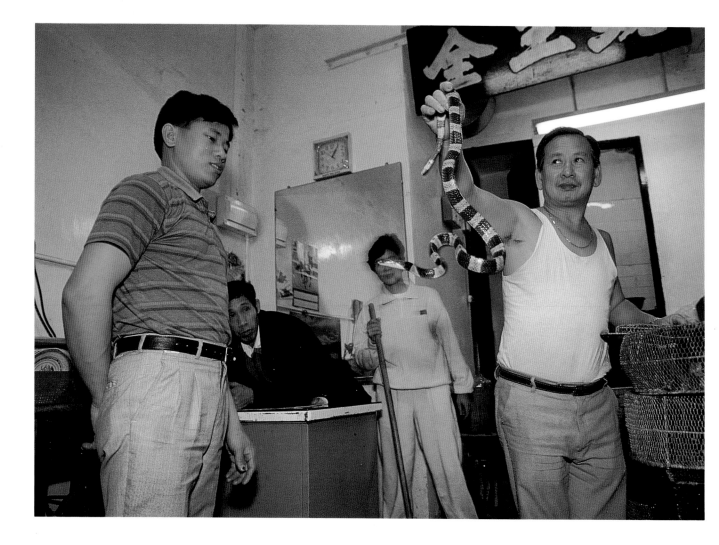

On Cleverly Street, a shop-keeper displays a banded krait, which, along with cobras, pythons, and rat snakes, are imported from China and Thailand for the neighborhood's snake restaurants; nearby Jervois Street is called "Snake Street." Soup and other types of snake dishes are particularly popular during the winter. According to traditional Chinese beliefs, snake meat heats the body and protects it from the cold (James Marshall).

A woman shakes a cup full of bamboo Qian sticks, each of which is numbered. The stick that falls out refers to a printed message concerning the fate of the young couple. Qian sticks are most often used to predict the results of school exams, prospects for success in business, and the likelihood that a new child will be a boy. Man Mo Temple on Hollywood Road is Hong Kong's oldest Buddhist temple; it is dedicated to Man, the god of literature, and Mo, the god of war (James Marshall).

WESTERN DISTRICT

81

A craftsman meticulously
carves the characters of a
name into a chop, or stamp.
It is difficult to do any type
of business in Hong Kong
without a chop, whose mark
functions in many business
transactions like a signature
does in the West. Chops are
made of ivory, bone, jade,
and various less expensive
stones (James Marshall).

TOP: *JJs in Wanchai is Hong Kong's hottest disco (James Marshall).*
MIDDLE: *The competition among Hong Kong's many karaoke clubs, where customers sing their favorite songs to accompanying instrumental melodies and background videos, has resulted in a few innovations. These include individual practice booths and TV screens in the rest rooms (Alex Webb).* BOTTOM: *Wanchai nightclubs employ young Filipinas who are carefully screened for beauty and poise. They work under rigid conditions and, when their short-term visas expire, they must return home. Despite conditions that make their lives like those of indentured servants, the money brings many back to Hong Kong repeatedly (James Marshall).*

■■

FACING PAGE: *Wanchai has changed since its nightlife was portrayed in the 1950s film* The World of Suzie Wong. *Foreigners frequenting the area today are just as likely to be attending a conference as searching for a wild night on the town (Rick Browne).*

HONG KONG

86

TOP: Steam rises from a chef's vat of noodles (Rick Browne). BOTTOM: Window shoppers inspect a display of gold jewelry and statues, particularly popular as wedding gifts. Chinese people have traditionally invested much of their savings in gold (Leong Ka Tai). LEFT: A woman gazes through the mist on a tram-car window on a rainy Wanchai day (Rick Browne).

■ ■

PAGES 88 AND 89: Window washers at work on the side of the New World Harbor View Hotel, 50 stories above Wanchai (Rick Browne).

Schoolchildren, like most people in Hong Kong, eat lunch and many other meals at sidewalk food stalls (Eli Reed).

FACING PAGE:
Sunset over Causeway
Bay's typhoon shelter
(Neil Farrin).

In Victoria Park, where
hundreds gather every morn-
ing to exercise and greet the
day, a woman practices tai
chi, *an ancient Chinese*
exercise (James Marshall).

A footpath off Stubbs Road,
which runs along the western
slope of Happy Valley, over-
looks the racecourse. Horse
racing is nearly an obsession
in Hong Kong, whose popula-
tion spends more on betting
at the races than it does on
income taxes (Alex Webb).

HONG KONG
94

*Land use is at a premium
in Hong Kong. The interior
of Happy Valley Racecourse
houses several soccer fields,
and the giant screen shows
results from daytime rac-
ing at Hong Kong's other
horsetrack at Sha Tin
(James Marshall).*

Company team members participate in a Walks for Millions event sponsored by the Community Chest, one of the many nongovernmental organizations that underwrite social welfare programs (Alex Webb).

FACING PAGE: China's treatment of its dissidents is a matter of concern for Hong Kong residents. In January 1991 hundreds of demonstrators protested the secret trials of China's democracy movement leaders (Eli Reed).

PAGES 98 AND 99: Mirrors—such as those in the lobby of a North Point movie house—are never used casually in Hong Kong because of the power accorded them by the principles of feng shui (Alex Webb).

A Cantonese opera star
takes a break backstage
before beginning a per-
formance at the Pearl
Theater in North Point
(Rick Browne).

*Yeung Lau Ching, a Hong
Kong opera star, performs at
the Sunbeam Theater. Like
most, she trained in China
(Neil Farrin).*

The tram line along King's Road runs between North Point and Quarry Bay (Alex Webb).

*ABOVE AND RIGHT: Six-
and seven-year-olds study
dance at the Jean Wong
School of Ballet in Quarry
Bay. Ballet lessons have
become popular among the
children of Hong Kong's
upwardly mobile middle
classes (James Marshall).*

■■

*PAGES 106 AND 107:
Boy Scouts, active in Hong
Kong since 1911, sell raffle
tickets to raise money for
charity outside the Quarry
Bay MTR Station
(James Marshall).*

FACING PAGE:
*The neon lights of Kowloon
color a cruise ship docked at
Ocean Terminal in shades of
pink (James Marshall).*

*A ferry passenger uses his
hour to read one of Hong
Kong's forty-plus daily
papers on the trip from
Cheng Chau to Hong Kong
(Susan Biddle).*

TOP: The Lamma Island ferry rounds the peninsula on the western side of Hong Kong (Robert Maass). *BOTTOM:* The Twinkling Star departs Kowloon for the crossing to Hong Kong Island. The Star Ferry Co., which operates 10 ships, has been carrying passengers across Victoria Harbor for nearly a century (Rob Nelson).

■■

FACING PAGE: In recognition of Hong Kong's role in maritime history, more than 100 Mexican navy cadets hung high from the rigging of the three-masted Cuauhtemoc when it sailed into Victoria Harbor as part of Mexico's celebration of its 180th anniversary of independence (Steve Stroud).

Night falls over Victoria Harbor as the sun settles behind the hills of Lantau Island (James Marshall).

■■

*FACING PAGE:
Junks with sails are rare today. The* Duk Ling, *a*

commercial junk, is one of the few (Rick Browne).

■■

*PAGES 114 AND 115:
A five-clawed dragon—usually representing Chinese emperors—adorns the Star Ferry building (Rob Nelson).*

A shopkeeper takes a tea
break in front of his Tsim
Sha Tsui shop. About 30
percent of the watches produced in Hong Kong are sold
in shops like these. The rest
are exported (Rick Browne).

■■

FACING PAGE:
An ivory importer and
former statue manufacturer

ponders the future of a
warehouse full of ivory that
cannot be sold. Although the
tusks were legally imported,
Hong Kong's compliance
with the international ivory
trade ban and a growing
world consciousness have
nearly destroyed its formerly
flourishing ivory arts
business (Rick Browne).

Tsim Sha Tsui has countless
shops selling jewelry, clothes,
and electronics (Alex Webb).
■■

FACING PAGE:
A homeless man in Tsim
Sha Tsui (Rob Nelson).

A makeup artist applies body paint to shoulders of dancers before a dress rehearsal of the Hong Kong Ballet (Susan Biddle).

FACING PAGE:
A principal ballerina performs with the Hong Kong Ballet at the Cultural Centre (Susan Biddle).

The comedy and kung-fu movie star Jackie Chan greets his fans at a gala charity preview of his latest film. These previews, for which tickets range from HK$300 to HK$1,000, are one way that Hong Kong charities raise money for their programs. But they do not bring in nearly as much money as the charity balls, which may charge more than HK$5,000 per ticket and can raise as much as HK$2.5 million in a single evening (James Marshall).

The socialite Diane Butler shares a private word with the pop singer Danny Chan at a movie fund-raising function. Chan is one of Hong Kong's top singing stars and has been creating hits for more than a decade. Butler, an Australian, man-aged to become a permanent fixture in the territory's often-closed high-society circles in less than five years. Many attribute her success to an ability to raise money and her ceaseless enthusiasm for charitable causes (James Marshall).

ABOVE AND FACING PAGE:
The entertainment at
Caesar's Nightclub, one of
many Japanese-style
nightclubs in Hong Kong,
ranges from the traditional
fan dance to erotic perform- *ances, catering to a variety*
of tastes. Club clients con-
sist primarily of foreign
businessmen, whose liberal
expense accounts can
finance a costly evening out
(Rick Browne).

Police arrest a shoplifter in a Tsim Sha Tsui department store scuffle. Crime, particularly burglary and theft, is on the rise in Hong Kong. The crimes are often committed by illegal immigrants who are smuggled by speedboat into the territory and then returned to China after the job is completed (Rick Browne).

Diners deliberate over a seafood selection at Yau Ma Tei's Temple Street night market stall. Open-air street restaurants, known as dai pai dongs, *are popular throughout Hong Kong (Robert Maass).*

FACING PAGE:
Temple Street also bustles with night-market shoppers in search of bargains. During the day, this street is full of automobile traffic and looks like any other in the area (Robert Maass).

A Yau Ma Tei sidewalk serves as the setting for a few serious games of pai-kau, *Chinese dominoes.*

■ ■

RIGHT: A fortune teller in the Temple Street night market.

PAGES 132 AND 133: The Yau Ma Tei typhoon shelter is home to many motorized fishing junks. With rare exception, the only junks that still use sails are commercially operated leisure craft (All, Robert Maass).

Freight handlers load boxes onto a lighter, or barge, that will take them to a waiting ship. About half of the cargo passing through Hong Kong Harbor is processed manually (Alex Webb).

FACING PAGE:
A fisherman repairs his net by hand. The fishing life has changed little, but many people are leaving their junks to live in new, government-built housing (Robert Maass).

*The corner of Jordan Road
and Nathan Road, in Yau
Ma Tei (Alex Webb).*

A seamstress sews sweaters at the Star Mills clothing factory in Hung Hom. Workers like these are usually paid by the piece; there is no minimum wage for ordinary Hong Kong workers (Rick Browne).

■■

FACING PAGE:
The workers of Sui Luen Jewelry Co. in Hung Hom, Kowloon, assemble necklaces. The factory produces both a standard line of products and custom jewelry (Rob Nelson).

*Around the corner from Bird
Street in Kowloon, people
meet to inspect and trade
songbirds. The singing ability of these birds is highly
valued by their Chinese
owners (James Marshall).*

Funerary shops sell paper houses, furniture, cars, money, and other objects that are ceremonially burned by Hong Kong people for use by their dead relatives in the next world (James Marshall).

PAGES 142 AND 143: Cricket owners stir up their insects in anticipation of another contest on Mong Kok's Bird Street. Money changes hands nearly as fast as the crickets can fight (Robert Maass).

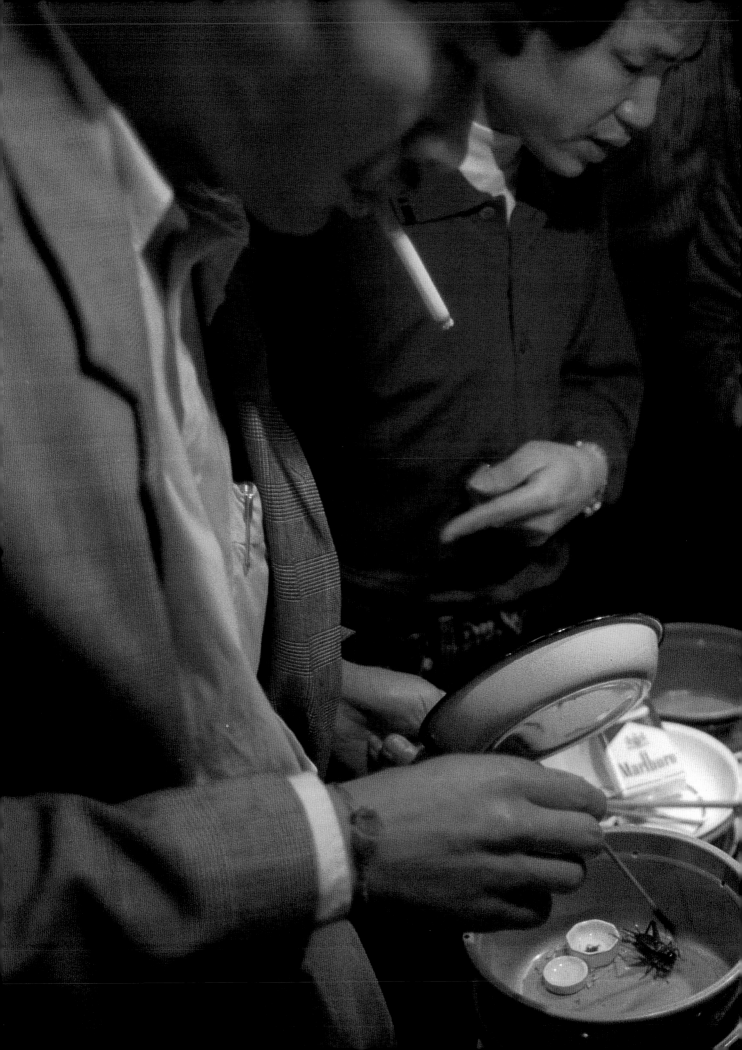

*The Convention of Peking,
which gave Britain its
hundred-year lease on the
New Territories until 1997,
reserved for China jurisdic-
tion over the old walled
Kowloon City. Chinese officials eventually abandoned it
and the Walled City became a
criminal hideout where colonial law was never enforced.
After World War II, squatters flooded in, and in the
1960s high-rises were built.
The streets of this impover-
ished slum are so narrow one
can touch the walls on both
sides, and there are tiny
heroin-processing factories,
criminals hiding from the
law, unlicensed dentists, and
illegal medical facilities.*

*The Walled City has long
been scheduled for demolition. Once the neighborhood
has been cleared, the eight-
acre site will be turned into
a park. For many children
who lived in the Walled
City, including nine-year-old
Yau Wing Tak, rooftops
were the only playground
(Eli Reed).*

KOWLOON

146

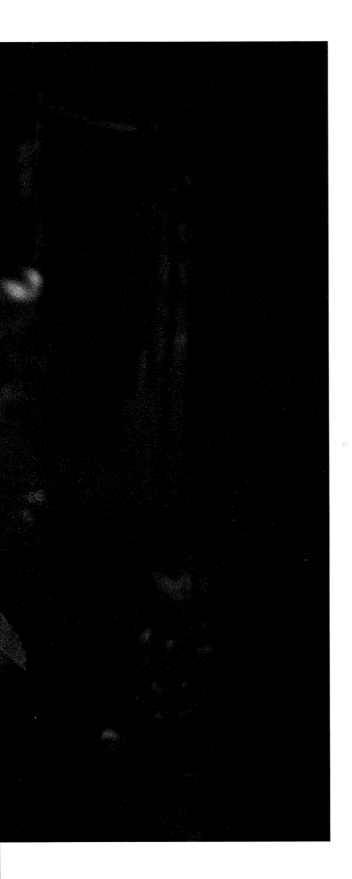

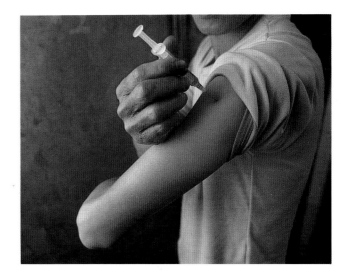

Because the Walled City was a no-man's land, the heroin trade flourished. At one time, drugs were bought and sold openly. LEFT: Former Triad member Peter Chan, now assistant manager in a restaurant, no longer lives in the Walled City but returns to try to help current gang members find another life (Both, Eli Reed).

*Can Hai Yuen, 69, operated a
grocery store in the Walled
City for 40 years (Eli Reed).*

Top: A back-alley chef creates stacks of traditional sweets. BOTTOM: A restaurant worker prepares duck eggs (Both, Eli Reed).

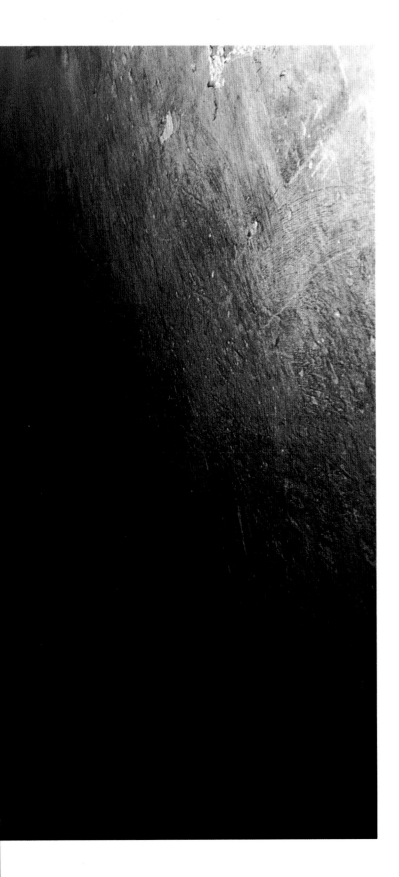

To outsiders, the Walled City was always an impenetrable maze (Eli Reed).

TOP: Dentists unable to get licenses in Hong Kong practiced in the Walled City. Ho Yin keeps watch over his children as he works. BOTTOM: Tong Sheung Yin and her daughter, Liu Hiu Ching, in their Walled City residence.

■■

FACING PAGE: Ho Yin's office was also his home (All, Eli Reed).

An apartment on the ground
floor of the Walled City
(Eli Reed).

*Little light penetrates the
crowded quarters of what
was known to the Cantonese
as the City of Darkness,
Hak Nam (Eli Reed).*

THE WALLED CITY

LEFT: *Kai Tak Airport buzzes with excitement as groups gather to bid their friends bon voyage (Jodi Cobb).* TOP: *Jumbo jets skim the tops of apartment buildings as they approach Kai Tak International Airport (Eli Reed).* BOTTOM: *A family begins a journey to a new life in Canada. More than 170 people emigrate from Hong Kong each day (Jodi Cobb).*

Many Hong Kong taxi drivers display their artistic creativity in dashboard decorations. Although they often use the opportunity to honor their favorite deity, others pay homage to such capitalistic icons as Mickey Mouse and McDonald's hamburgers (Jodi Cobb).

FACING PAGE TOP: Restaurants are at the heart of social life in Hong Kong because most apartments are too small for entertaining. Customers of the Teck Hsin Fire Pot Restaurant in Kowloon cook portions of their dinner at their table (Robert Maass).

FACING PAGE BOTTOM: Hong Kong's Golden Harvest Films is the producer of kung fu and science fiction films as well as the Ninja Turtles movies (Jodi Cobb).

■■

*PAGES 160 AND 161: Two police officers stop a young woman to check her identifi-*cation card, a document that must be carried by every Hong Kong resident at all times. During regular street patrols, law enforcement officials search for illegal immigrants and gang members. It is illegal to be a gang member in Hong Kong (Rob Nelson).

CHAI WAN

159

Teenagers perform stunts at a housing area in Chai Wan. Hong Kong has more than 70 such temporary facilities for residents who have lost homes because of urban renewal or natural disasters but have lived in Hong Kong less than seven years (Leong Ka Tai).

■ ■

FACING PAGE:
Ching Ming is a Confucian spring festival during which Hong Kong people visit the graves of their dead relatives to offer flowers, food, and gifts to the spirits. As part of the festivities, families may have a picnic at the grave site (Rick Browne).

Inside the Sau Mau Ping housing estate. Teenagers, especially those from poorer families, are tempted by gang membership for its promise of economic improvement (Basil Pao).

■■

LEFT: *A dragon drapes itself over the shoulders of a young man in Sau Mau Ping. Gang members are known to decorate their bodies with elaborate tattoos (Basil Pao).*

Diners deliberate over the makings for their meal in the market at Lei Yue Mun, a village of seafood restaurants. Once a decision is made, the selected items will be delivered to the chef of the restaurant in which they wish to eat (Leong Ka Tai).

A grocery boat delivers supplies, including canned goods and fresh fruits, to a junk anchored in Aberdeen Harbor (Rob Nelson).

■ ■

FACING PAGE:
About 500 junks make their home in the harbor of Aberdeen on Hong Kong Island. Each junk usually has several bedrooms, a kitchen, a hold for storing fish, and its own generator. Boat people are members of the Tanka and Hoklo ethnic groups, and many have never had a home on land (Jodi Cobb).

British soldiers of the Royal Regiment of Wales stationed in Hong Kong's Fort Stanley carry on colonial tradition as they participate in the annual inspection of the regimental silver. Through each piece, they learn the history of the battles and operations of their battalion (Rob Nelson).

FACING PAGE:
A young acrobat from China performs at Middle Kingdom, a historical theme park in the Ocean Park recreation area. The Hong Kong Tourist Association has encouraged the development of such attractions so that visitors will extend their stay (James Marshall).

Taffy, the mascot goat of the Royal Regiment of Wales, poses with her master, whose only responsibilities are to see that she is fed, groomed, and dressed properly for military functions (Rob Nelson).
RIGHT: Part of the Repulse Bay Lifeguard Club, built in the style of a Chinese temple (Alex Webb).

■■

PAGES 174 AND 175: An Ocean Park visitor observes a shark overhead in the underwater aquarium (Jodi Cobb).

Joseph Yu exemplifies the hardworking Hong Kong entrepreneur. His Chinese name, Pak Chin, means "100 wholes" or, as he says, "I've got everything." He works four jobs, gets only a few hours of sleep many nights, and shares a 120-square-foot room with his wife and two sons. He is a hospital telephone operator several nights a week, teaches kung fu to children, owns a chauffeur service with his sister, and fills in driving a taxi when needed. Insightful, witty, and intelligent, Joseph has devoted himself to creating a better life for his sons. "Life is like a piece of paper," he says. "You have to write something or draw something or put some colors on it to make it look beautiful. Once I die my boys and the people in the world will look at my paper and say, 'That's what he did.' Everything is on that piece of paper."

■■

TOP LEFT AND RIGHT: On a typical day, Joseph bids his son farewell and chauffeurs a bride and groom as they make the obligatory wedding-day calls on their parents (Jodi Cobb). BOTTOM RIGHT: He decorates his Mercedes for the couple (Jodi Cobb). BOTTOM LEFT: Joseph drove a taxi full-time for seven years but stopped because the pay was low, taxi rental high, and diesel fuel expensive. Now he co-owns a Mercedes (Susan Biddle).

TOP: Joseph and his wife practice martial-arts moves at a playground while their sons look on (Jodi Cobb). BOTTOM: Joseph teaches martial arts to young boys from his neighborhood and nearby housing estates. After studying with his own master for more than a decade, Joseph is now known as the "little master." (Jodi Cobb).

*Joseph, his wife, Winnie
Wong Yuk Ping, and their
sons live in a room in his
wife's family's apartment in
Pok Fu Lam while they await
new housing (Jodi Cobb).*

*Joseph breakfasts on a bowl
of congee, or rice porridge,
as a pig is delivered to market (James Marshall).*

Because there is no room in the urban centers of Hong Kong and Kowloon, bike clubs take their cycles to the outer islands for weekend excursions. Hong Kong's growing affluence has allowed for leisure activities that the parents of these athletes could not have imagined in their youth (Rick Browne).

LANTAU ISLAND

*A man pedals his bicycle
down a quiet side street in
Tai O, a fishing village
on Lantau Island
(Rick Browne).*

FACING PAGE:
*The world's largest outdoor
sitting Buddha blesses Po
Lin Monastery on Lantau
Island (Neil Farrin).*

Drying fish hang over a Tai O street. Unlike most Lantau islanders, who are farmers, the people of Tai O have traditionally earned their living from the sea. Many of them are members of the Tanka ethnic group, known as boat people because they have always lived aboard junks. Their current homes of landed junks or houses built on stilts are scheduled to be torn down by the government because of poor health conditions: houses on stilts dump sewage directly into the water (Rick Browne).

■ ■

*FACING PAGE:
Chow Mei Ling, 63, operates a sampan water taxi in Tai O Bay (Rick Browne).*

Two Vietnamese children stare out from the Hei Ling Chau Detention Center at a world they have yet to experience. This detention center, located off the coast of Lantau Island, houses Vietnamese who have been declared illegal immigrants, rather than political refugees, and those who have not yet been classified.

■ ■

LEFT: Vietnamese asylum-seekers head for lunch (Both, Rick Browne)

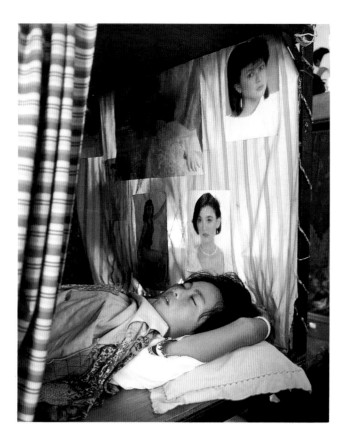

TOP: A teenager sleeps beneath the faces of fashion models. BOTTOM: A primary-school student studies her Vietnamese language lesson. RIGHT: Cubicles house whole families and their possessions.

■ ■

PAGES 190 AND 191: Sampans crowd the Cheung Chau waterfront (All, Rick Browne).

A rural resident makes his way down an overgrown path. Although the center of Cheung Chau is crowded with shops and small apartment buildings, tiny vegetable farms are tucked away in the quiet countryside (James Marshall). *RIGHT:* The goddess Kun Iam, the Queen of Heaven, is tattooed on a man's back (Rick Browne).

A shopkeeper rests for a few moments to read the newspaper (Basil Pao).

■ ■

PAGES 194 AND 195: A bamboo-balancing construction worker slowly makes his way up a steep Cheung Chau back street (Susan Biddle).

A second-grade student at the Cheung Chau Fisheries Joint Association School listens to his teacher. More than 90 percent of the students in this school are the children of the boat people whose junks make their home in the Cheung Chau harbor (Susan Biddle).

TOP: Fisheries school students share a comic book before class. BOTTOM: Second-graders clown for the camera.

■ ■

PAGES 198 AND 199: Four friends gather for a game of Mah-Jongg. The four players who participate in a Mah-Jongg game draw and discard plastic tiles until one gets the required combinations and wins (All, Susan Biddle).

*Worshippers offer prayers
and incense at Pak Tai
Temple on Cheung Chau
(Alex Webb).*

Scores of high-rise hous-
ing blocks transformed
Sha Tin from a sleepy
farming village to a bus-
tling new town in less than
a decade. Sha Tin is one
of eight new towns created
in the New Territories by
the government that are
now home to 37 percent of
the population.

■ ■

FACING PAGE:
*Yaohan is one of several
department stores that cater
to the commuters who have
settled in Sha Tin (All,
Rick Browne).*

A horse at the Sha Tin Racecourse is given a thorough shower after emerging from the equine swimming pool. Animals who are exercised in the pool are usually suffering from such ailments as tendinitis. The horses that compete at Hong Kong's two racecourses are very carefully cared for, and for good reason. One June 1991 race alone brought in more than US$16 million in gross receipts, a record for Hong Kong (Susan Biddle).

The eyes of the crowd are focused on the leading horse in a race at Sha Tin. Although most race-goers hope to benefit themselves, a portion of the profits made by the Royal Hong Kong Jockey Club is used to operate hospitals, clinics, parks, swimming pools, and other facilities, thus benefiting all of Hong Kong (Robert Maass).

■ ■

PAGES 206 AND 207: A worker in a Cheung Sha Wan garment factory that makes blue jeans (Alex Webb).

Sunday is family day in Hong Kong. A Tai Wai amusement area, a concrete expanse the size of three football fields, has arisen in the midst of Tai Wai's high-rise housing estates. Bicycle-cart rental stalls line the perimeter, and an amusement park is located on its edge (James Marshall).

A watchmaker carefully assembles watches at Gordon See & Co. in Kwai Chung. Hong Kong ranks as the world's largest exporter of watches (Robert Maass).

*Trucks load containers each
night at the Hong Kong
International Container
Terminal. Hong Kong com-
petes with Singapore for the
status of world's busiest container port (Alex Webb).*

KWAI CHUNG

211

LEFT AND BOTTOM: A pig farmer inspects his heat-lamp-treated piglets and a Hakka woman inspects her vegetables at the Kadoorie Farm in the Lam Tsuen Valley. The farm was created in the early 1950s by the wealthy Kadoorie family to help poor Chinese immigrants learn to make a living from the land (Susan Biddle).

■ ■

PAGES 214 AND 215: A worker at the San Miguel Brewery in Sham Tseng in the New Territories pours hops into copper cookers. San Miguel vies with China's Tsing Tao as the favorite local beer (Susan Biddle).

Hakka women of three-century-old Kat Hing Wai carry on a rural life-style in one of Hong Kong's few remaining walled villages. The ethnic group known as Hakka lived isolated from the other peoples of southern China. The mainstream Han Chinese looked down upon the Hakka, partly because they refused to bind the feet of their women and considered them to be equal partners in agricultural endeavors (Alex Webb).

A woman rounds the corner of a narrow alley in Kat Hing Wai village (Alex Webb).

■■

PAGES 218 AND 219: A woman takes a rest at Ching Chung Koon Temple in Tuen Mun. The names and photographs of the dead, as well as flowers, adorn the walls of its ancestral hall. This Taoist temple also offers subsidized rooms to 140 poor elderly people who have no place else to live (Alex Webb).

TOP: A junk sails into Tolo Harbor (Neil Farrin).
BOTTOM: A woman and her child look at the rowboats for rent at Port Shelter (Neil Farrin).

■■

FACING PAGE:
A bulldozer clears land for more housing blocks near Ma On Shan in the New Territories (Neil Farrin).

The marine police nightly patrol Hong Kong waters in search of smugglers. The two-way traffic in smuggled commodities—consumer goods to China and drugs, prostitutes, and gangsters to Hong Kong—has become a serious problem. Smuggling boats are specially built and fitted with four high-powered outboard motors; they are far faster than patrol boats. According to a marine police officer, each of the three branches of coastal authority in the People's Republic is in collusion with a different group of smugglers (James Marshall).

A Hong Kong police boat
stops a Chinese Territory
Vessel (CTV) to search for
illegal immigrants. CTVs
are not allowed to enter
Hong Kong waters except in
special cases, such as when
the passengers need emer-
gency medical treatment or
emergency food or water
supplies. Even then, they
must first be cleared by the
immigration department
(James Marshall).

TOP: The High Island Detention Center is situated on a strip of land next to a reservoir on the Sai Kung peninsula. BOTTOM: The residents of High Island live in metal Quonset huts, awaiting an uncertain future. Prior to June 16, 1988, all Vietnamese arrivals were declared refugees and eligible for resettlement abroad. A steady and increasing stream proved a strain on Hong Kong—the prison system administers the detention centers—and now arrivals are screened. If Hong Kong declares them refugees, they are placed in open camps where they can come and go as they please. Approximately one in twelve achieve this status. If they are classified as illegal immigrants, they go to detention centers like this one to await repatriation to Vietnam (Both, Jodi Cobb).

TOP: Teachers take High Island nursery school children out to play. BOTTOM: Vietnamese asylum seekers line up for lunch (Both, Leong Ka Tai).

CLOCKWISE FROM TOP LEFT: A woman is served food by workers at the High Island Detention Center. Residents collect their ration of rice. Vietnamese asylum-seekers spend many years living in sleeping cubicles. Hanging decorations adorn a bunk-bed shrine; many of the residents are devout Roman Catholics (All, Leong Ka Tai).

*TOP AND MIDDLE:
Primary-school students,
many of whom will spend
six to ten years in the camp,
study hard, not knowing
where their lives will take
them (Leong Ka Tai).
BOTTOM: A young student
completes her homework
in her home, a cubicle
(Leong Ka Tai).*

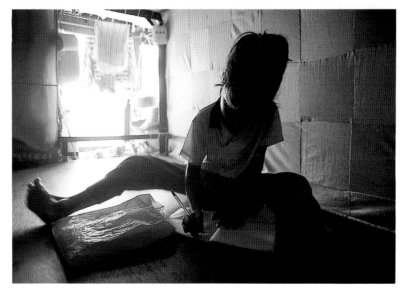

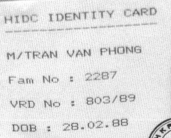

HIDC IDENTITY CARD   5207

M/TRAN VAN PHONG

Fam No : 2287

VRD No : 803/89

DOB : 28.02.88

TOP: A Vietnamese family registers for a visit to the clinic (Leong Ka Tai). BOTTOM: The various sections of High Island Detention Center are separated by guarded gates (Leong Ka Tai).

FACING PAGE: Three-year-old Tran Van Phong displays her identity card (Leong Ka Tai).

The town houses and condo-miniums of Club Marina Cove at Hebe Haven have been designed to serve as a weekend retreat for Hong Kong's wealthy elite (Neil Farrin).

LEFT: The 20,000 residents of Fairview Park, a private housing development near Yuen Long in the New Territories, have created a Westernized middle-class life-style quite different from that of their fellow Hong Kongers (Jodi Cobb). TOP: A family's weekend chores are like those in suburbs all over the world (James Marshall). BOTTOM: A resident repairs the Fairview Park version of a white picket fence (James Marshall).

TOP: A barge carrying construction materials cruises through the Sham Chun, or Shen Zhen, River, a no-man's-land that marks the Chinese border. BOTTOM: The border fence doubles as an active, though illegal, black-market trading post for useful goods not easily available in China (Both, Basil Pao).

Just across the Chinese border, the special economic zone of Shen Zhen waits to merge with Hong Kong after 1997 (Basil Pao).

ACKNOWLEDGMENTS

T HERE ARE MANY individuals who gave generously of themselves to this publication, and to both those named and those not named, we want you to know that without your help there would be no book.

In Hong Kong, which truly became our second home during the course of this project, there are many we wish to recognize. The list must begin with Ying Price, Chief of the Foreign Commercial Service of the U.S. Consulate, whose enthusiasm and dynamic personality breathed the final breath of life into our book. Hers is a friendship we will long cherish. To Patricia Davis, our principal on-site editor, who endured untold hours of research before our photographers arrived and survived the often chaotic methods by which we implemented this project, we send our heartfelt gratitude.

Dubravka Bondulic, the national photo editor at *Newsweek*, came to Hong Kong and immediately brought a much needed level of expertise, insight, and professionalism to our project. Steve Stroud, photo editor of the *South China Morning Post* and a key member of our production team, gave up his vacation to participate in the making of the book and contributed his personal knowledge of the inner workings of the city. Emmy Lung, whose gentle, gifted, and resilient ways became familiar to our entire group and who personifies much of what we have grown to admire in the people of

this city, facilitated our contact with the people of Hong Kong in myriad ways.

Our relationship with Po Chung, the personable chairman of DHL International, exemplifies the nature of our rapport with the community of Hong Kong. After listening to our explanation of the proposed book he immediately became one of our strongest partners and was a major factor in making the book a reality. Our enduring gratitude goes to Robert Lam (Robert Lam Color Labs), who personally orchestrated the creation of the elegant color prints of our photographers' work, which was beautifully displayed in Pacific Place. Thanks also to Swire Group for use of this magnificent venue. We thank Debbie Biber, Shelley Bird, Cassandra Orange (all of Hill & Knowlton) and Judi Arundel (Hotel Conrad Public Relations) for their innumerable suggestions and wise counseling. We also want to express our appreciation to Melina Hung and Douglas King (Hong Kong Tourist Association) for listening to our concept in the very earliest stages and in being among the first to give us their support.

We would be remiss if we did not add to the list of those we thank the names of Linda Rose (*Hong Kong Standard*); John Dykes (*South China Morning Post*); Tom Darmody (Greiner-Maunsell); Karisa Lui, Stephen Wong, and Penny Byrne (all from HKTA Hong Kong); Winnie Pau (Shangri-La

Hotel); Lillian Chang (Peninsula Hotel Group); Anders Poon (Kowloon Hotel); Nina Bindra (Park Lane Hotel); Edward Lee (Robert Lam Color Labs); Dorothy Chan Lai Lai (our most patient office assistant); and Judy Fung and Wendy Lo (Profile Hong Kong). We wish to thank Akin Lai, Ivan Lau, Michael Yeung, and Edmund Chan, our tireless photographers' assistants. Stephen Wong (Apple Computer), Chris Banakis (Motorola), and Daniel Ng (McDonalds) were all most generous and helped our endeavors immensely.

A very special thank you is reserved for Maureen Graney, senior editor at Stewart, Tabori & Chang, who has contributed more than she can imagine to this book. We also owe a great deal to publisher Andy Stewart, who put his faith in us, and to Diana Jones, Sarah Longacre, and the entire staff for their superb craftsmanship. We cannot thank Simon Winchester enough for his probing and timely introduction, which gives a special dimension to this book. And our heartiest appreciation goes to Judy Jacobs for her commitment in so carefully crafting the captions which enlighten each of the photographs in this book.

Mary Bahkt (HKTA New York) has given us her friendship and shown unending faith in our concept. Guy Cooper, picture editor of *Newsweek*, contributed years of experience and savvy to editing the seventy thousand images that we produced into the best, which you see here. And on two coasts, Melinda Parsons in San Francisco (Hong Kong Government Information Service) and Sarah Monks in New York (Hong Kong Trade Development Council) have contributed considerably to this endeavor. In Hong Kong, Mark Pinkstone and Cynthia Lockeyear (both of the Hong Kong Government Information Service) assisted us immeasurably with fact-finding and providing access to key individuals.

We are forever indebted to the sponsors who backed this enterprise with the funding needed to do the job right. We send our sincerest appreciation to: AT&T's Simon Kreiger and Joe Berrier for their enthusiastic backing; Po Chung and Andy Tseng of DHL International for their patronage and friendship; the entire staffs of Hill & Knowlton Asia Ltd. and the Hong Kong Tourist Association; and Robert Woo and Dario Regazzoni of the shiny new Hotel Conrad Hong Kong, who were among the earliest to stand behind our endeavor and treated us all to the finest views of Victoria Harbor.

Kodak (Far East) Ltd., through photo products manager Doug Seator, sales promotion coordinator Tim Cheung, Charles Leung, and their hardworking staff, deserves special thanks for going way overboard in their assistance and help in setting up our public seminar, photo exhibition, and for providing classy jackets to the team. Retired vice president and general manager Ray DuMoulin of the Professional Photography Division of Eastman Kodak Company was one of the cornerstones of this project and got us underway with his blessing and plenty of good Kodak film.

John Detweiler, James Clark, RM Navalenko, and Jane Lau from Mobil Oil Hong Kong Ltd. encouraged and supported our efforts and hosted our entire group to a delightful farewell dinner in the breathtaking setting of the Tai Tam American Club. Northwest Airlines' John Watkins, Albert Lau, and June Sage Chan flew our team of editors and photographers to Kai Tak airport safely and in supreme comfort in their 747 airplanes. And Robert Shamis of Wishbone Trading Co., Ltd., believed in our dream and dug into his budget. Many, many thanks to these generous individuals and corporations.

Of course, without the energy, creativity, and talents of our photographers, we would not have been able to bring the story of the people of Hong Kong to life. We hope each of them understands the important contribution they have made and how much their involvement has meant to us.

And finally we owe a very personal thank you to Kathy Browne and Maurine Marshall, who encouraged us, believed in us, worried with us, and who helped make our dream come true, and it is with them that we gladly share our triumph.

—*R. B.* and *J. M.*

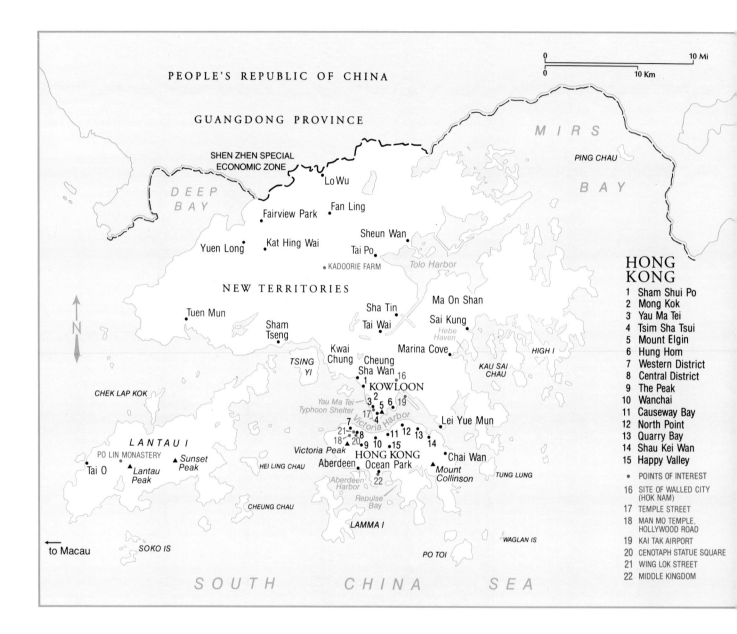

PEOPLE'S REPUBLIC OF CHINA

GUANGDONG PROVINCE

SHEN ZHEN SPECIAL
ECONOMIC ZONE

MIRS

PING CHAU

*DEEP
BAY*

Lo Wu

Fan Ling

Fairview Park

BAY

Yuen Long

Kat Hing Wai

Sheun Wan

Tai Po

Tolo Harbor

• KADOORIE FARM

NEW TERRITORIES

Tuen Mun

Sha Tin

Ma On Shan

Sham
Tseng

Tai Wai

Sai Kung

*Hebe
Haven*

Kwai
Chung

Marina Cove

HIGH I

CHEK LAP KOK

*TSING
YI*

Cheung
Sha Wan

*KAU SAI
CHAU*

16

1

KOWLOON

*Yau Ma Tei
Typhoon Shelter*

3   2
5   6   19
17
4

Lei Yue Mun

7

Victoria Harbor

LANTAU I

21
18 20
8
9   10

11 12 13
15

14

PO LIN MONASTERY

Victoria Peak

HONG KONG

Chai Wan

Tai O

▲ *Lantau
Peak*

▲ *Sunset
Peak*

HEI LING CHAU

Aberdeen   Ocean Park

▲ *Mount
Collinson*

TUNG LUNG

22

*Aberdeen
Harbor*

*Repulse
Bay*

CHEUNG CHAU

LAMMA I

WAGLAN IS

to Macau

SOKO IS

PO TOI

SOUTH   CHINA   SEA

HONG
KONG

1   Sham Shui Po
2   Mong Kok
3   Yau Ma Tei
4   Tsim Sha Tsui
5   Mount Elgin
6   Hung Hom
7   Western District
8   Central District
9   The Peak
10 Wanchai
11 Causeway Bay
12 North Point
13 Quarry Bay
14 Shau Kei Wan
15 Happy Valley

•   POINTS OF INTEREST
16 SITE OF WALLED CITY
    (HOK NAM)
17 TEMPLE STREET
18 MAN MO TEMPLE,
    HOLLYWOOD ROAD
19 KAI TAK AIRPORT
20 CENOTAPH STATUE SQUARE
21 WING LOK STREET
22 MIDDLE KINGDOM

HONG KONG

ABOUT THE PHOTOGRAPHERS

Susan Biddle (The White House, Washington) is an official White House photographer who travels regularly with President Bush. She also freelances for many newspapers, magazines, and wire services, and has been a staff photographer at the *Denver Post* and *Topeka Capitol-Journal*. Ms. Biddle began her career as director of photography for the Peace Corps. (*Pages 12–13, 66, 74–75, 109, 120, 121, 176 bottom left, 194–195, 196, 197 top and bottom, 198–199, 204, 212–213, 213, 214–215.*)

Rick Browne (co-founder, Pacific Rim Concepts, San Francisco) is a travel and feature photographer who works with *People, Life, Time, Newsweek, Forbes, Travel Age West, Canadian, Tours & Resorts,* and *Endless Vacation* as well as with corporations and public-relations agencies. His work is represented by SIPA Press, Stock Boston, and The Stock Broker. In 1991 he received the Portfolio/Silver Award in the American Society of Travel Writers' Photographer of the Year contest. (*Pages 26, 29, 33, 58 bottom, 73, 85, 86–87, 87 top, 88–89, 100, 112, 116, 117, 124, 125, 126–127, 138, 162, 180–181, 182, 184, 185, 186–187, 187, 188 top and bottom, 188–189, 190–191, 192 right, 202, 203 left and right.*)

Jodi Cobb (*National Geographic,* Washington) began her career with the *Wilmington* (Delaware) *News-Journal* and the *Denver Post* and now is a staff photographer for *National Geographic.* That magazine has published her photo essays on New York's Broadway and women of Saudi Arabia, among other topics. She has won many photographic awards, including Pictures of the Year category awards, a World Press Award, and was the first woman named White House News Photographers Association's Photographer of the Year. (*Pages 6–7, 18–19, 20, 31, 53, 58 top, 67, 156–157, 157 bottom, 158, 159 bottom, 168, 174–175, 176 top left, top right, and bottom right, 177 top and bottom, 178, 224 top and bottom, 232–233.*)

Neil Farrin (Pro-File, Hong Kong) is an editorial and corporate photographer who owns and operates Pro-File, an international photo agency. He and his agency complete assignments for Asian and North American magazines, public relations firms, advertising agencies, and the travel industry. (*Pages 11, 14–15, 28, 32, 48, 92, 101, 183, 220 top and bottom, 221, 230–231.*)

Leong Ka Tai (Camera 22 Ltd., Hong Kong) began his career in Paris. Mr. Leong is a regular contributor to *Geo, Stern, Paris Match,* and *National Geographic,* for whom he recently completed an extensive project in China. He was the photographer for Ken Hom's *A Taste of China,* and has contributed to more than a dozen other books including *The Long March* and *Singapore: Island City, State.* (*Pages 45, 58 middle, 59, 72, 87 bottom, 163, 166–167, 225 top and bottom, 226 all, 227 all, 228, 229 top and bottom.*)

Robert Maass (SIPA Press, New York) is a contract photographer for *Newsweek* who has traveled extensively through Eastern Europe, Africa, Nicaragua, and the Sudan on assignment. He has also worked for ABC television and the *New York Times* and has two children's books to his credit: *Firefighters* and *When Autumn Comes.* (*Back cover, pages 44, 56, 57, 68, 110 top, 128, 129, 130, 130–131, 132–133, 134, 142–143, 159 top, 205, 210.*)

James Marshall (co-founder, Pacific Rim Concepts, New York) is a travel photojournalist whose clients include public relations firms, tourism boards, and numerous magazines including *Newsweek, Smithsonian, Bon Appetit, Endless Vacation,* and *Diversion.* His photographs are syndicated through The Stock Market and JB Pictures. He was the organizer of "Document Brooklyn," a project in which forty-five photographers captured one week in the life of Brooklyn, New York; it resulted in a major exhibition and an as-yet unpublished book. (*Front cover, pages 2–3, 8, 30, 60–61, 62–63, 76, 77 top and bottom, 78 top and bottom, 78–79, 80, 81, 82–83, 84 top and bottom, 93, 95, 104, 104–105, 106–107, 108, 113, 122, 123, 140, 141, 171, 179, 192 left, 208–209, 222, 223, 233 top and bottom.*)

Rob Nelson (Black Star, Atlanta) is a contract photographer for *Newsweek* covering the southern United States. He freelances for *Business Week, Forbes, Fortune,* and *USA Today* and photographs annual reports for a number of major US corporations. (*Pages 9, 49, 69, 110 bottom, 114–115, 119, 139, 160–161, 169, 170, 172.*)

Basil Pao (Treasure Art Ltd., Hong Kong) has worked for *AsiaWeek, Discovery, Rolling Stone,* the *New York Times Magazine,* and *Playboy,* and he has had books on China and Indonesia published. Mr. Pao was the still photographer for the film *The Last Emperor.* (*Page 21, 22, 23, 43, 70–71, 164–165, 165, 193, 234 top and bottom, 235.*)

Eli Reed (Magnum, New York) was awarded the 1982 Neiman Fellowship at Harvard, and was given the World Understanding, Overseas Press Club, and World Press Awards for his coverage of Central America. He covered the U.S. invasion of Panama for *Life* and frequently works with *Parenting, Hippocrates,* and the *New York Times Magazine.* His book, *Beirut: City of Regrets,* was published in 1988, and another book, about Black America, is forthcoming. (*Pages 64, 64–65, 90–91, 96, 144–145, 146–147, 147, 148, 149 top and bottom, 150–151, 152, 153 top and bottom, 154, 155, 157 top.*)

Alex Webb (Magnum, New York) works with *Life,* the *New York Times Magazine, Geo,* and *National Geographic* as well as other magazines. Mr. Webb has had two books published, *Hot Light/Half-Made Worlds: Photographs from the Tropics* and *Under a Grudging Sun: Photographs from Haiti Libere 1986–1988.* He has exhibited his photographs in museums and galleries throughout the world and was included in the Whitney Biennial in 1991. (*Pages 4–5, 27, 38, 39, 84 middle, 94, 97, 98–99, 102–103, 118, 135, 136–137, 172–173, 200–201, 206–207, 211, 216, 217, 218–219.*)

The type in this book was set in Cochin with Adobe Garamond Titling Capitals, composed in-house on the Macintosh IIsi in QuarkXpress 3.0, and output on the Linotronic L300 at The Sarabande Press, New York, New York.

The book was printed and bound by Toppan Printing Co. (H.K.) Ltd., Quarry Bay, Hong Kong.